The Ultimate Plant Based Cookbook for Beginners

500 Quick and Easy Recipes for Busy People and 21-Day Meal Plan to Reset and Energize Your Body

By
Nicki Lawrence

© Copyright 2021 by Nicki Lawrence- All rights reserved.

This document is geared towards providing exact and reliable information in regards to the topic and issue covered. The publication is sold with the idea that the publisher is not required to render accounting, officially permitted, or otherwise, qualified services. If advice is necessary, legal or professional, a practiced individual in the profession should be ordered.

- From a Declaration of Principles which was accepted and approved equally by a Committee of the American Bar Association and a Committee of Publishers and Associations.

It is not legal in any way to reproduce, duplicate, or transmit any part of this document in either electronic means or in printed format. Recording of this publication is strictly prohibited and any storage of this document is not allowed unless with written permission from the publisher. All rights reserved.

The information provided herein is stated to be truthful and consistent, in that any liability, in terms of inattention or otherwise, by any usage or abuse of any policies, processes, or directions contained within is the solitary and utter responsibility of the recipient reader. Under no circumstances will any legal responsibility or blame be held against the publisher for any reparation, damages, or monetary loss due to the information herein, either directly or indirectly.

Respective authors own all copyrights not held by the publisher.

The information herein is offered for informational purposes solely, and is universal as so. The presentation of the information is without contract or any type of guarantee assurance.

The trademarks that are used are without any consent, and the publication of the trademark is without permission or backing by the trademark owner. All trademarks and brands within this book are for clarifying purposes only and are the owned by the owners themselves, not affiliated with this document.

Table of contents

INTRODUCTION 4

CHAPTER 1: UNDERSTANDING THE BASICS OF PLANT-BASED DIET   5

1.1 Different Types of Plant-Based Diet 5

1.2 Benefits of Plant-Based Diet 5

CHAPTER 2: GETTING STARTED WITH THE DIET 8

2.1 21-Days Sample Meal Plan for Plant-Based Diet 8

2.2 Plant-Based Diet- Shopping List 13

CHAPTER 3: HEALTHY BREAKFAST RECIPES FOR PLANT-BASED DIET   14

3.1 Plant-Based Breakfast Recipes 14

CHAPTER 4: PLANT-BASED SALAD, APPETIZERS, AND SNACKS   36

4.1 Appetizer Recipes 36

4.2 Snacks Recipes 55

4.3 Salad Recipes 71

CHAPTER 5: DELICIOUS PLANT-BASED LUNCH AND DINNER RECIPES   87

5.1 Vegan Oil-Free Lunch and Dinner Recipes 87

5.2 Grains Recipes for Lunch and Dinner 99

5.3 Wraps and Burgers Recipes 110

5.4 Soups and Bowls Recipes 120

CHAPTER 6: PLANT-BASED SWEETS AND SIDE DISHES 131

6.1 Desserts and Sweets 131

6.2 Side Dishes 147

CONCLUSION 163

Introduction

Plant or plant-based diet relies mainly on plant-derived foods. This includes not only fruit and veggies but also nuts, seeds, fats, full grains, legumes including beans. It does not mean that you are vegan or vegetarian or you do not eat meat and milk. Alternatively, you pick more of your ingredients correspondingly from plant sources. Plant-based, whole-food eating is better than you thought. Full grains, potatoes and beans are some of the most inexpensive bulk foods you can find. Build menus around these staple foods, and you will probably spend less on a meat-rich diet and other animal products than you do.

Moving to a plant-based diet is one of the most critical moves you can take to enhance your health, energy levels and decrease the chance of chronic diseases. There is excellent scientific evidence that many chronic illnesses can be managed, decreased or even reversed by switching to a plant-based diet focused on whole food. The study shows that a plant-based diet can reduce the risk of developing diabetes, heart attacks, some forms of cancer, and other significant diseases.

You will need to prepare a little ahead, but finding whole-food, plant-based meals on the go is pretty straightforward. Fruits and dishes made with pasta, rice, and potatoes can typically be found wherever you are. You can also cook some delicious food with little innovation and versatility while travelling far. Plant-based foods contain all of the vital nutrients that we need (excluding vitamin B12). You can get some B12 from fortified foods like plant-based milk and breakfast cereals, but a precise B12 supplementation is the best source.

People adopting vegan diets do not consume any animal products, including dairy, meat, poultry, seafood, chickens and honey. Vegetarians remove from their diets all meat and poultry, but some vegetarians consume eggs, fish or dairy. In comparison, the plant-based diet is more versatile. One person may consume no animal products following a plant-based diet, and another may eat small amounts of poultry, eggs, seafood, and meat.

Starting with a plant-based diet, this book will help you to create and schedule your diet with 21-days meal plan and shopping list. Benefits of a plant-based diet and a basic understanding of this diet is discussed to make you confident of your choice. This book also includes breakfast recipes, lunch and dinner recipes, appetizers, snacks, sweets, desserts, salads and side dishes based on plant food.

Chapter 1: Understanding the Basics of Plant-Based Diet

Shifting to a plant-based diet does not only support the health, but it may even help to reduce risk of many diseases. People that adopt plant-based diets seem to have lower impacts on the environment. Adopting healthy eating practices will help decrease the production of greenhouse gases, water usage, and land used for industrial farms, both influences in global warming and other environmental deterioration.

An analysis of sixty-three studies found that diets consuming the least amount of animal-based ingredients, such as dairy, vegetarian and vegan diets, have had the most health advantages. The study estimated that a seventy percent reduction in greenhouse gases and land use and a fifty percent reduction in water usage could be accomplished by changing Western diet trends to healthy dietary habits focused on plants.

1.1 Different Types of Plant-Based Diet

People follow a plant-based diet for a range of factors including animal care issues, nutritional problems, environmental issues or appetite and social pressures. Plant-based diets are becoming increasingly common and can promote healthier living at all ages and stages of life if well organized. Plant-based diet types might include:

Lacto-Ovo Vegetarians

They eat eggs and dairy foods but not beef, poultry or fish.

Lacto-Vegetarians

They eat animal product but do not consume milk, beef, poultry or fish.

Vegans

They eat no agricultural goods, including milk, butter and poultry, at all. Many shops have ready-made items' stock which include animal ingredients, so it is essential to read the labels on all packaged goods carefully.

Ovo-Vegetarians

They have eggs but exclude all other feeding kinds of stuff, including beef.

1.2 Benefits of Plant-Based Diet

There are many benefits when a person starts taking a plant-based diet. It can help you to lose your weight, obesity, can increase your heart life, can boost your cognitive ability, diabetes control and prevent other cancer-causing symptoms. Adopting a plant-based whole-food diet not only increases your waistline but will also reduce the incidence and minimize the effects of some chronic diseases.

Lose Weight and Improve Health

Obesity is an increasing phenomenon of proportion. More than sixty-nine per cent of adults in the United States are overweight or obese. Fortunately, improving the diet and lifestyle will make weight control possible and have a positive effect on wellness. Research has found that diets focused on vegetables are effective for weight loss. In addition to the absence of delicate items, the high fibre quality of the plant-based diet is a good recipe for losing extra pounds.

Adopting a balanced eating strategy based on vegetables will also help to hold the weight off for the long term. Merely taking out artificial items that are not tolerated on a plant-based diet such as soda, sweets, fast food, and refined grains is often a good weight loss technique.

Reduce Risk of Cancer

Research indicates you can reduce the risk of certain types of cancer after a plant-based diet. An analysis of more than sixty-nine thousand people showed that vegetarian diets were correlated with a substantially lower rate of intestinal cancer, especially for those adopting a vegetarian Lacto-Ovo plan. Another primary research of more than seventy-seven thousand people found that non-vegetarians have a twenty-two percent smaller chance of contracting the cardiovascular disease than those who adopted vegetarian diets. Vegetarians consuming fish, have the best defense against colon cancer with a decreased incidence of forty-three percent compared to non-vegetarians.

Prevent Cognitive Decline

Some research indicates diets high in vegetables and fruits may help decrease or delay cognitive deterioration in older adults and Alzheimer's disease. Food diets include a more significant amount of plant compounds and nutrients, which have been proven to slow Alzheimer's disease growth and reverse memory impairment. Increased levels of fruits and vegetables have been closely linked with a decrease in cognitive impairment in several experiments.

Reduce Risk of Diabetes

Adopting a plant-based diet may be an essential way to control and reduce the risk of diabetes progression. A research performed in over two-million people showed that those that adopted a balanced plant-based diet had a thirty-four percent reduced chance of developing diabetes than others who ate poor, non-plant-based diets.

Another research found that plant-based diets were correlated with almost a fifty percent decrease in the cases of diabetes relative to non-vegetarian diets. In addition, plant-based diets were shown to boost blood sugar regulation in people living with diabetes.

Healthy Heart

The most well-known advantages of plant-based diets are perhaps that people with plant-based diet have healthy heart. A recent analysis of over two million people showed that those eating a balanced plant-based diet high of herbs, tomatoes, entire-grains, legumes and nuts have a slightly lower chance of contracting heart failure relative to those adopting non-plant-based diets. When adopting a plant-based diet, eating the correct kinds of food is crucial to avoiding heart failure, which is why staying true to a plant-based diet is the safest option.

Chapter 2: Getting Started with the Diet

Before you get started with your plant-based diet, you need to schedule your daily meal and need to do some shopping while keeping in mind the essential and necessary ingredients for your plant-based diet. Here are the 21-days sample meal plan and a shopping list to ease your work and save time.

2.1 21-Days Sample Meal Plan for Plant-Based Diet

Here is a 21-days sample meal list for you to get started with plant-based diet.

Day 1
Appetizer: Smoky Portobello Tacos
Breakfast: Orange French Toast
Lunch: Vegan Spinach Artichoke Dip + Warm Japanese Yam and Shiitake Salad
Snacks: Spicy Peach Salsa
Dinner: The Ultimate Vegetable Vegan Lasagna + Potato Korokke

Day 2
Appetizer: Buffalo Tempeh Tacos
Breakfast: Chocolate Chip Coconut Pancakes
Lunch: Vegan Cauliflower Soup + Sprouting Broccoli Salads
Snacks: Early Spring Pesto
Dinner: Vegan Tomato Basil Soup + Fab cakes

Day 3
Appetizer: Mexican Molletes
Breakfast: Chickpea Omelets
Lunch: Soba Noodle Bowl + Crispy Lemon Tofu
Snacks: Spicy Grapefruit Margarita
Dinner: Vegan Baked Ziti + Quinoa Fried Rice

Day 4

Appetizer: Corn and Crab Dumplings

Breakfast: Apple-Lemon Bowl

Lunch: Easy Lemon Rosemary White Bean Soup + Autumn Crunch Salads

Snacks: Lemon Meringue Pie

Dinner: Mexican Walnut Meat + Yaki Onigiri

Day 5

Appetizer: Beluga Lentil Tacos

Breakfast: Brown Rice Breakfast Pudding

Lunch: Vegan Pozole + Mexican Cobb Salads

Snacks: Cauliflower Blueberry Smoothie

Dinner: Tomatillo Salsa Verde + Cauliflower Spare Ribs

Day 6

Appetizer: Grape Leaf Mezze Bowls

Breakfast: Breakfast Scramble

Lunch: Enchilada Rice + Curried Chickpea Salads

Snacks: Stuffed Mushrooms

Dinner: Herbed Barley Bowl + Greek Pasta Salad

Day 7

Appetizer: Mexican Black Bean Skillet

Breakfast: Black Bean and Sweet Potato Hash

Lunch: Italian Walnut Meat + Grilled Caesar Salad

Snacks: Minted Hot Chocolate

Dinner: American Walnut Meat + Happy Pancake

Day 8

Appetizer: Loaded Summer Bratwursts

Breakfast: Apple-Walnut Breakfast Bread

Lunch: Curried Chickpea Salad + Harvest Bowls

Snacks: Silky Chocolate Mousse

Dinner: Loaded Sweet Potato Nachos + Cranberry Walnut Vegan Chicken Salad

Day 9

Appetizer: Fiesta Enchilada Skillet

Breakfast: Mint-Chocolate Green Protein Smoothie

Lunch: Vegan Goulash + Chopped Greek Salads

Snacks: Ranch Roasted Nuts

Dinner: Stuffed Acorn Squash with Quinoa + Toasted Quinoa Stir-Fry

Day 10

Appetizer: Mediterranean Flatbreads

Breakfast: Vegan Salmon Bagel

Lunch: Vegan Butternut Squash Mac and Cheese + Crispy Lemon Tofu

Snacks: Salted Almond Thumbprint Cookies

Dinner: Curried Blistered Green Beans with Orange Rice + Sweet Corn Risotto

Day 11

Appetizer: Crispy Black Bean Tacos

Breakfast: Dairy-Free Coconut Yoghurt

Lunch: Stuffed Poblano Chiles + Spanish-Style Tofu

Snacks: Molasses Crinkle Cookies

Dinner: Spicy Tomato Sushi Rolls + Spring Radish Fattoush

Day 12

Appetizer: Pulled BBQ Jackfruit Sandwiches

Breakfast: Vegan Green Avocado Smoothie

Lunch: Sopes with Beans and Corn + Italian Chopped Salads

Snacks: Chocolate Peanut Butter Pie

Dinner: Quick Brown Rice Congee + Crispy Turnip Cakes

Day 13

Appetizer: Carrot Socca Cakes

Breakfast: Sun-Butter Baked Oatmeal Cups

Lunch: Green Beans and Potatoes with Mustard Vinaigrette + Brassica Bowls

Snacks: Vegan Eggnog

Dinner: Grits and Greens + Tempura Sweet Potato Bao

Day 14

Appetizer: Italian Chopped Salads

Breakfast: Chocolate Peanut Butter Shake

Lunch: Thai Rice Salad Bowls + Thai-Style Broccoli Salad

Snacks: Mango Drink

Dinner: Forbidden Rice Bowl with Quick-Pickled Cabbage + Southern Spoonbread

Day 15

Appetizer: Black Bean Avocado Melts

Breakfast: Chipotle Black Bean Avocado Toast

Lunch: Farro, Mushroom, and Leek Gratin + Rainbow Salads

Snacks: Peanut Butter Sesame Cookies

Dinner: Herbed Instant Pot Rice Pilaf + Okonomiyaki

Day 16

Appetizer: Super Green Breakfast Sandwiches

Breakfast: Breakfast Panini

Lunch: Easy Turmeric Eggplant Curry + Kale Salads

Snacks: Fresh Fruit and Coconut Popsicles

Dinner: Caribbean Rice + Sweet Potato Chaat

Day 17

Appetizer: Falafel

Breakfast: Blueberry Lemon French Toast

Lunch: Costa Rican Rice and Beans + Thai Mango Salads

Snacks: Classic Coleslaw

Dinner: Peach and Pepper Tacos + Spicy Almond Butter Odon

Day 18

Appetizer: Caper Dill Bagels

Breakfast: Antioxidant Blueberry Smoothie

Lunch: Jackfruit Barbecue Sandwiches with Broccoli Slaw + Chopped Salad

Snacks: Crunchy Winter Vegetable Salad

Dinner: Zoodle Rolls with Pesto Sauce + Cornmeal Arepas

Day 19

Appetizer: Figgie Grilled Cheese Sandwiches

Breakfast: Chewy Oatmeal Banana Pancakes

Lunch: Veggie Summer Rolls + Roasted Roots Salads

Snacks: Matcha Earth Bites

Dinner: Curried Millet Sushi + Grilled Corn and Cherry Tomato Salsa

Day 20

Appetizer: Korean Tofu Tacos

Breakfast: No-Bake Vegan Breakfast Cookies

Lunch: Buffalo Cauliflower Pita Pockets + Chopped Salads with Avocado

Snacks: Cashew and Dried Cherry Granola

Dinner: Tortilla Roll-Ups with Lentils and Spinach + Winter Chowder

Day 21

Appetizer: Jackfruit Tacos

Breakfast: Zucchini Bread Baked Oatmeal

Lunch: Five-Ingredient Veggie Burger + Antipasto Salad

Snacks: Miso Power Dressing

Dinner: Sloppy Joe Pitas + Creamy Coconut Carrot Soup

2.2 Plant-Based Diet- Shopping List

To follow a plant-based diet, you need to do shopping to buy ingredients for your daily meal. Here is a shopping list to ease your task.

- **Whole Grains**

Brown rice, farro, quinoa, rolled oats, barley, brown rice pasta, etc.

- **Fruits**

Berries, peaches, pears, pineapple, citrus fruits, bananas, etc.

- **Starchy Vegetables**

Potatoes, butternut squash, sweet potatoes, etc.

- **Vegetables**

Kale, spinach, cauliflower, broccoli, asparagus, carrots, peppers, tomatoes, jalapeno, lettuce, etc.

- **Legumes**

Peas, peanuts, lentils, chickpeas, black beans, etc.

- **Healthy Fats**

Avocados, coconut oil, olive oil, unsweetened coconut, etc.

- **Unsweetened Plant-Based Milk**

Coconut milk, cashew milk, almond milk, etc.

- **Plant-Based Protein**

Tofu, plant-based protein powders or sources, tempeh.

- **Seeds, Nuts and Nut Butter**

Almonds, tahini, pumpkin seeds, macadamia nuts, sunflower seeds, cashews, natural peanut butter, etc.

- **Condiments**

Salsa, nutritional yeast, mustard, soy sauce, lemon juice, vinegar, etc.

- **Spices, Herbs and Seasonings**

Basil, turmeric, salt, curry, rosemary, black pepper, etc.

- **Beverages**

Coffee, sparkling water, tea.

Chapter 3: Healthy Breakfast Recipes for Plant-Based Diet

Conversely, a "plant-based" diet relies on balanced, unrefined or minimally modified plant-sourced items (nuts, beans, herbs, berries, vegetables, grains) and few animal-based goods such as free-range chickens, natural poultry or fish species. A plant-based diet focuses on natural grains and unprocessed choices, intending to consume whole grains and so much of it. If you are adopting a plant-based diet, or just searching for more vegetables to consume, so there is no better time to start than breakfast. These recipes leverage the plant's nutritional properties to prepare your day for a healthy start.

3.1 Plant-Based Breakfast Recipes

Here are many plant-based breakfast recipes that are affordable and are easy to prepare in less time.

ORANGE FRENCH TOAST

Cooking Time: 30 Minutes

Serving Size: 8 Slices

Calories: 480

Ingredients:

- 2 cups of plant milk (unflavored)
- Four tablespoon maple syrup
- 1½ tablespoon cinnamon
- Salt (optional)
- 1 cup flour (almond)
- 1 tablespoon orange zest
- 8 bread slices

Method:

1. Turn the oven and heat to 400°F afterwards.
2. In a cup, add ingredients and whisk until the batter is smooth.
3. Dip each piece of bread into the paste and permit to soak for a couple of seconds.
4. Put in the pan, and cook until lightly browned.

5. Put the toast on the cookie sheet and bake for ten to fifteen minutes in the oven, until it is crispy.

CHOCOLATE CHIP COCONUT PANCAKES

Cooking Time: 30 Minutes

Serving Size: 8 Pancakes

Calories: 95

Ingredients:

- 1¼ cup oats
- 2 teaspoons coconut flakes
- 2 cup plant milk
- 1¼ cup maple syrup
- 1⅓ cup of chocolate chips
- 2¼ cups buckwheat flour
- 2 teaspoon baking powder
- 1 teaspoon vanilla essence
- 2 teaspoon flaxseed meal
- Salt (optional)

Method:

1. Put the flaxseed and cook over medium heat until the paste becomes a little moist.
2. Remove seeds.
3. Stir the buckwheat, oats, coconut chips, baking powder and salt with each other in a wide dish.
4. In a large dish, stir together the retained flax water with the sugar, maple syrup, vanilla essence.
5. Transfer the wet mixture to the dry ingredients and shake to combine
6. Place over medium heat the nonstick grill pan.
7. Pour ¼ cup flour onto the grill pan with each pancake, and scatter gently.
8. Cook for five to six minutes, before the pancakes appear somewhat crispy.

CHICKPEA OMELET

Cooking Time: 30 minutes

Serving size: 3 omelets for 3 persons

Calories: 290

Ingredients:

- 2 cup flour (chickpea)
- 1½ teaspoon onion powder
- 1½ teaspoon garlic powder
- ¼ teaspoon pepper (white and black)
- 1/3 cup yeast
- 1 teaspoon baking powder
- 3 green onions (chopped)

Method:

1. In a cup, add the chickpea flour and spices.
2. Apply 1 cup of sugar, then stir.
3. Power medium-heat and put the frying pan.
4. On each omelets, add onions and mushrooms in the batter while it heats.
5. Serve your delicious Chickpea Omelet.

APPLE-LEMON BOWL

Cooking Time: 15 minutes

Serving Size: 1-2 servings

Calories: 331

Ingredients:

- 6 apples
- 3 tablespoons walnuts
- 7 dates
- Lemon juice
- ½ teaspoon cinnamon

Method:

1. Root the apples, then break them into wide bits.
2. In a food cup, put seeds, part of the lime juice, almonds, spices and three-quarters of the apples. Thinly slice until finely ground.
3. Apply the remaining apples and lemon juice and make slices.

BREAKFAST SCRAMBLE

Cooking Time: 30 minutes

Serving Size: 6 servings

Calories: 320

Ingredients:

- 1 red onion1 to
- 2 tablespoons soy sauce
- 2 cups sliced mushrooms
- Salt to taste
- 1½ teaspoon black pepper
- 1½ teaspoons turmeric
- ¼ teaspoon cayenne
- 3 cloves garlic
- 1 red bell pepper
- 1 large head cauliflower
- 1 green bell pepper

Method:

1. In a small pan, put all vegetables and cook until crispy.
2. Stir in the cauliflower and cook for four to six minutes or until it smooth.
3. Add spices to the pan and cook for another five minutes.

BROWN RICE BREAKFAST PUDDING

Cooking Time: 15 minutes

Serving Size: 4 servings

Calories: 400

Ingredients:

- 2 cups almond milk
- 1 cup dates (chopped)
- 1 apple (chopped)
- Salt to taste
- ¼ cup almonds (toasted)
- 1 cinnamon stick
- Ground cloves to taste
- 3 cups cooked rice
- 1 tablespoon raisins

Method:

1. Mix the rice, milk, cinnamon stick, spices and dates in a small saucepan and steam when the paste is heavy.
2. Take the cinnamon stick down. Stir in the fruit, raisins, salt and blend.
3. Serve with almonds bread.

BLACK BEAN AND SWEET POTATO HASH

Cooking Time: 30 minutes

Serving Size: 4

Calories: 280

Ingredients:

- 1 cup onion (chopped)
- ⅓ Cup vegetable broth
- 2 garlic (minced)
- 1 cup cooked black beans
- 2 teaspoons hot chili powder

- 2 cups chopped sweet potatoes

Method:

1. Put the onions in a saucepan over medium heat and add the seasoning and mix.
2. Add potatoes and chili flakes, then mix.
3. Cook for around 12 minutes more until the vegetables are cooked thoroughly.
4. Add the green onion, beans, and salt
5. Cook for more 2 minutes and serve.

APPLE-WALNUT BREAKFAST BREAD

Cooking time: 60 minutes

Serving Size: 8

Calories: 220

Ingredients:

- 1½ cups apple sauce
- ⅓ cup plant milk
- 2 cups all-purpose flour
- Salt to taste
- 1 teaspoon ground cinnamon
- 1 tablespoon flax seeds mixed with 2 tablespoons warm water
- ¾ cup brown sugar
- 1 teaspoon baking powder
- ½ cup chopped walnuts

Method:

1. Preheat to 375°F.
2. Combine the apple sauce, sugar, milk, and flax mixture in a jar and mix.
3. Combine the flour, baking powder, salt, and cinnamon in a separate bowl.
4. Simply add dry ingredients into the wet ingredients and combine to make slices.
5. Bake for 25 minutes until it becomes light brown

VEGAN SALMON BAGEL

Cooking time: 30 minutes

Serving size: 2

Calories: 430

Ingredients:

- 4 cups of water
- 1½ red onion
- vegan cream cheese
- salt, pepper
- 4 bagels
- 1½ cup of apple cider vinegar
- 7 carrots

Method:

1. Preheat to 200°C.
2. Slice the carrots.
3. In a mixer to mix, combine sugar, vinegar, and ground pepper.
4. Put the carrot strips in a stir fry bowl, apply the marinade and stir.
5. Cover the carrots with foil and bake for twenty minutes, then switch heat down to 210°F and cook for 40 minutes more.

MINT CHOCOLATE GREEN PROTEIN SMOOTHIE

Cooking time: 10 minutes

Serving size: 1

Calories: 440

Ingredients:

- 1 scoop chocolate powder
- 1 tablespoon flaxseed
- 1 banana
- 1 mint leaf
- ¾ cup almond milk

- 3 tablespoons dark chocolate (chopped)

Method:

1. Blend all the ingredients except the dark chocolate.
2. Garnish dark chocolate when ready.

DAIRY-FREE COCONUT YOGURT

Cooking time: 10 minutes

Serving size: 2

Calories: 180

Ingredients:

- 1 can coconut milk
- 4 vegan probiotic capsules

Method:

1. Shake coconut milk with a whole tube.
2. Remove the plastic of capsules and mix in.
3. Cut a 12-inch cheesecloth until stirred.
4. Freeze or eat immediately.

VEGAN GREEN AVOCADO SMOOTHIE

Cooking Time: 10 minutes

Serving size: 2

Calories: 400

Ingredients:

- 1 banana

- 1 cup water
- ½ avocado
- ½ lemon juice
- ½ cup coconut yoghurt

Method:
1. Blend all ingredients until smooth.

SUN-BUTTER BAKED OATMEAL CUPS

Cooking Time: 35 minutes

Serving Size: 12 cups

Calories: 300

Ingredients:
- ¼ cup coconut sugar
- 1½ rolled oats
- 2 tablespoon chia seeds
- ¼ teaspoon salt
- 1 teaspoon cinnamon
- ½ cup non-dairy milk
- ½ cup Sun-Butter
- ½ cup apple sauce

Method:
1. Preheat oven to 350°F.
2. Mix all ingredients and blend well.
3. Add in muffins and Insert extra toppings.
4. Bake 25 minutes, or until golden brown.

CHOCOLATE PEANUT BUTTER SHAKE

Cooking Time: 5 minutes

Serving Size: 2

Calories: 330

Ingredients:
- 2 bananas
- 3 Tablespoons peanut butter
- 1 cup almond milk
- 3 Tablespoons cacao powder

Method:
1. Combine ingredients in a blender until smooth.

CHIPOTLE BLACK BEAN AVOCADO TOAST

Cooking Time: 15 minutes

Serving size: 4

Calories: 290

Ingredients:
- 2 pieces of toast
- 1 tsp of garlic powder
- Salt to taste
- 1 can of black beans
- 1 avocado
- ¼ a cup of corn
- 3 tablespoon red onion (chopped)
- ¼ a tsp of chipotle spice
- black pepper to taste
- 1 lemon juice
- ½ tomato

Method:
2. Combine rice, chipotle sauce, garlic, salt, pepper and ½ lime juice.
3. Boil about 15 minutes.
4. Combine coriander, onion, ½ lime juice and spices.

5. Toast slices of bread and put black bean on the toast.
6. Garnish with mashed avocado.

BREAKFAST PANINI

Cooking Time: 5 minutes

Serving Size: 1

Calories: 450

Ingredients:

- ¼ cup of raisins
- 1 tablespoon cinnamon
- 3 teaspoon cacao powder
- ¼ cup peanut butter
- 1 banana
- 3 slices of bread

Method:

1. Add raisins, the ¾ cup hot water, cinnamon and cocoa powder.
2. Cut the banana and put on toast with peanut butter.
3. Blend the raisins and cut them into sandwiches.

BLUEBERRY LEMON FRENCH TOAST

Cooking Time: 30 minutes

Serving Size: 2-3

Calories: 500

Ingredients:

- 2 tablespoon flaxseed in hot water
- 1 cup of milk

- 8 slices of bread
- Salt to taste
- 1 cup of blueberries
- 1 teaspoon of vanilla extract
- 1 teaspoon of cinnamon
- ½ lemon juice
- 1-2 tablespoon of maple syrup

Method:
1. Mix and blend all ingredients except bread and blueberries.
2. Soak the whole grain bread in the batter, and fried at low heat.
3. Flip the toast until crusted, and dark the other hand.
4. Sprinkle with blueberry syrup when ready.

ANTIOXIDANT BLUEBERRY SMOOTHIE

Cooking Time: 5 minutes

Serving Size: 2

Calories: 220

Ingredients:
- 1 cup blueberries
- 1 cup almond milk
- ½ avocado
- Salt to taste
- 1 banana

Method:
1. Blend ingredients together until smooth

CHEWY OATMEAL BANANA PANCAKES

Cooking Time: 10 minutes

Serving Size: 8

Calories: 450

Ingredients:

- 1 ½ cups oats
- 3 ripe bananas
- 6 dates
- 1 cup non-dairy milk
- Salt to taste
- 3 tablespoons chia seeds
- 1 teaspoon cinnamon

Method:

1. Blend all ingredients until smooth.
2. Make low heat pancakes so as not to stick and cook until deep brown.

NO-BAKE VEGAN BREAKFAST COOKIES

Cooking Time: 25 minutes

Serving Size: 8-10

Calories: 350

Ingredients:

- 1 cup dates
- ½ cup flaxseed
- ¼ cup chocolate chips
- ¼ cup nuts
- 2 cups oats
- ¾ cup nut butter
- 2 tablespoons maple syrup

Method:

1. Soak dates in water for 10 minutes.
2. Mix dry ingredients in a bowl.
3. Blend soft dates and maple syrup until smooth.

4. Mix remaining ingredients with dates and dry paste.
5. Take the dough and give cookie shapes.

ZUCCHINI BREAD BAKED OATMEAL

Cooking Time: 30 minutes

Serving Size: 1

Calories: 190

Ingredients:
- 1 tablespoon raisins
- Salt to taste
- ¼ teaspoon nuts
- ½ teaspoon cinnamon
- ½ cup rolled oats
- ¼ teaspoon baking powder
- ½ teaspoon vanilla extract
- ¼ cup non-dairy milk
- ½ cup zucchini

Method:
1. Preheat your oven to 350°F.
2. Mix all dry ingredients
3. Mix the wet ingredients separately.
4. Mix dry and wet ingredients.
5. Bake for 18-20 minutes.

CHOCOLATE SMOOTHIE WITH FROZEN CAULIFLOWER

Cooking Time: 10 minutes

Serving Size: 2

Calories: 400

Ingredients:

- 1 cup cauliflower
- 2 bananas
- 2 cups of milk
- 2 dates
- 2 tablespoons peanut butter
- 3 tablespoons cocoa powder

Method:

1. Mix all ingredients and blend until smooth.

CHOCOLATE CHERRY ZUCCHINI SMOOTHIE

Cooking Time: 5 minutes

Serving Size: 2

Calories: 380

Ingredients:

- 1 medium zucchini
- 2 tablespoons almond butter
- 1 cup almond milk
- 2 tablespoons cocoa powder
- 1 cup cherries
- 1 teaspoon vanilla extract

Method:

1. Place all ingredients and blend until smooth.

CHOCOLATE BLACK BEAN SMOOTHIE

Cooking time: 5 minutes

Serving Size: 2

Calories: 362

Ingredients:

- 1½ cup soy milk
- 1 tablespoon cashew butter
- 2 bananas
- 2 tablespoons cocoa powder
- ½ cup black beans
- 4 dates

Method:

1. Place all of the ingredients in mixer and blend until smooth.

HEALTHY MOCHA SMOOTHIE

Cooking Time: 15 minutes

Serving Size: 1-2

Calories: 300

Ingredients:

- 1 banana
- ¼ cup dates
- ¾ cup milk
- ¼ cup strong coffee
- 1½ tablespoon cocoa powder

Method:

1. Mix all ingredients in mixer and blend until smooth.

PAPAYA DATE SMOOTHIE

Cooking Time: 5 minutes

Serving Size: 2

Calories: 350

Ingredients:

- 2 cups papaya
- 2 bananas
- 3 dates
- 1½ cups milk

Method:

1. Mix all of the items in mixer and blend until smooth.

HEALTHY FRUIT CEREAL

Cooking Time: 10 minutes

Serving Size: 1

Calories: 344

Ingredients:

- 1 cup milk
- 1 cup berries
- 1 tablespoon of oats
- 1 banana
- 1 tablespoon of dried fruit
- Cinnamon to taste

Method:

1. Place fruit into a bowl.
2. Pour milk over the top.

PEANUT BUTTER BANANA AND GRANOLA TOAST

Cooking Time: 5 minutes

Serving Size: 4

Calories: 180

Ingredients:

- 4 piece of bread
- 3 tablespoons peanut butter
- 1½ ripe banana
- Granola to require
- Cinnamon to taste
- maple syrup 1 teaspoon

Method:
1. Toast the bread and put other ingredients as toppings.
2. Add seasoning and serve.

CREAMY SWEET POTATO TOAST

Cooking time: 5 minutes

Serving Size: 4

Calories: 160

Ingredients:
- 4 piece of bread
- 2½ cup sweet potato
- 2½ tablespoon tahini
- Pumpkin seeds

Method:
1. Toast the bread and put ingredients.
2. Add spices and serve with juice.

AVOCADO TOAST

Cooking Time: 5 minutes

Serving Size: 4

Calories: 170

Ingredients:

- 4 piece of bread
- 2¼ avocado
- 2½ tablespoon yeast
- Salt to taste
- black pepper to taste

Method:
1. Toast the bread and put ingredients.
2. Add spices and serve with smoothie.

CHOCOLATE COCONUT WITH NUTS TOAST

Cooking Time: 5 minutes

Serving Size: 4

Calories: 180

Ingredients:
- 4 piece of bread
- Chocolate Peanut Butter
- Coconut
- Hazelnuts

Method:
1. Toast the bread and put toppings.
2. Add seasoning and serve.

BERRY-BERRY SMOOTHIE

Cooking Time: 5 minutes

Serving Size: 1

Calories: 320

Ingredients:
- two cups of rice milk

- one banana
- ½ cup blueberries
- ¼ cup raspberry juice.

Method:
1. Put all the ingredients in a blender and mix until smooth.

GINGER PEACH SMOOTHIE

Cooking Time: 5 minutes
Serving Size: 1
Calories: 300

Ingredients:
- 1½ cups peaches
- 2 dates
- 2 cup almond milk
- ½ cup yoghurt
- 1½ teaspoon flaxseeds
- 1½ banana
- ½ teaspoon ginger
- 1 tablespoon honey
- Salt to taste

Method:
1. Combine the ingredients in a blender and mix until smooth.

Fruit Cereal

Cooking Time: 10 minutes
Serving Size: 1
Calories: 152

Ingredients:
- ¼ cup dried fruit
- 1 cup fresh berries

- 3 bananas
- 3 dates
- 1 apple

Method:

1. Place the sliced fresh fruits and dried fruit in a bowl.
2. Blend banana in water to reach your desired consistency for a banana milk.
3. Pour over fruit.

APPLE BANANA NO-OATMEAL

Cooking Time: 5 minutes

Serving Size: 1

Calories: 170

Ingredients:

- ¼ cup raisins
- 4 bananas
- 6 dates
- 3 apples
- Cinnamon to taste

Method:

1. Blend fruits.
2. Pour in bowl and top with raisins.

AVERAGE SMOOTHIE

Cooking Time: 5 minutes

Serving Size: 1

Calories: 400

Ingredients:

- 1 banana

- 1½ cup cherries
- 2 mangoes
- ⅛ teaspoon vanilla extract

Method:
1. Blend all ingredients until smooth.

BERRY POMEGRANATE BOWL

Cooking Time: 5 minutes

Serving Size: 1

Calories: 144

Ingredients:
- 2 bananas
- 4 dates
- 1½ cup berries
- 1 pomegranate
- ½ cup raspberries
- 1 tablespoon chia seeds

Method:
1. Blend fresh fruits.
2. If desired, add water and serve.

Chapter 4: Plant-Based Salad, Appetizers, and Snacks

This chapter will cover the plant-based salads recipes, appetizer recipes and snack recipes to fill your day with nutritious food.

4.1 Appetizer Recipes

SMOKY PORTOBELLO TACOS

Cooking Time: 30 minutes

Serving Size: 2

Calories: 430

Ingredients:

- ½ cup of rice
- 8 Portobello mushrooms
- 1 garlic clove
- 1 lime, radish and jalapeno
- 1 tablespoon liquid smoke
- 4 corn tortillas
- 2 red cabbage
- Salt and pepper

Method:

1. Boil the rice and heat oven at 400°F for tortillas.
2. Cut vegetables and mushrooms. Cook mushrooms on low heat until brown.
3. Blend jalapeno with lime juice and spices to make the sauce.
4. Wrap tortilla with rice, sauce and vegetables.

BUFFALO TEMPEH TACOS

Cooking Time: 30 minutes

Serving Size: 2

Calories: 325

Ingredients:

- ⅓ Cup hot sauce
- 2 tablespoon butter
- 2 scallions
- 4 radishes
- 6 corn tortillas
- 8 oz. tempeh

Method:

1. Make buffalo tempeh in butter and hot sauce and bake on 375°F.
2. Prepare vegetables in olive oil and vinegar.
3. Wrap tortillas with sauce and tempeh.

MEXICAN MOLLETES

Cooking Time: 35 minutes

Serving Size: 2

Calories: 380

Ingredients:

- 2 torta rolls
- 2 radishes
- tomato
- lime
- red onion
- lettuce
- jalapeño

Method:

1. Bake torta rolls on 450°F and cut the vegetables.

2. Cook on low heat with chipotle and mozzarella.
3. Serve torta with vegetables.

CORN & CRAB DUMPLINGS

Cooking Time: 45 minutes

Serving Size: 2

Calories: 320

Ingredients:

- ½ cup of sushi rice
- 2 scallions
- 1 corn
- 2 tablespoon cream cheese
- 14 dumpling wrap
- 2 teaspoon tamari

Method:

1. Cook rice and prepare the seasoning for dumplings filling.
2. Fill and cook dumplings in oil for 2 minutes.
3. Serve with sauce.

BELUGA LENTIL TACOS

Cooking Time: 30 minutes

Serving Size: 2

Calories: 360

Ingredients:

- ⅔ cup beluga lentils
- 1 packet vegetable broth
- 2 radishes
- 1 jalapeño and lime

- 1 avocado
- ½ teaspoon chipotle powder
- 6 corn tortillas
- 4 oz. cabbage

Method:
1. Cook lentils on 330°F and prepare vegetables in oil.
2. Make Chipotle and jalapeno slaw and adding seasonings.
3. Serve with sauce.

GRAPE LEAF MEZZE BOWLS

Cooking Time: 15 minutes

Serving Size: 2

Calories: 340

Ingredients:
- 8.8 oz. rice
- 2 cucumbers
- 2 radishes
- 4 tomatoes
- 6 grape leaves

Method:
1. Heat rice in the oven for 1 minute and prepare seasonings.
2. Serve with sauce and vegetables.

MEXICAN BLACK BEAN SKILLET

Cooking Time: 25 minutes

Serving Size: 2

Calories: 255

Ingredients:

- 8 oz. brown rice
- 4 oz. tomatillos
- 1 lime
- 2 garlic cloves
- 1 onion
- 1 bell pepper
- 13.4 oz. black beans
- 1 cheddar cheese

Method:

1. Prepare and Cook tomatillos salsa.
2. Prepare and cook vegetables.
3. Cook skillets with black beans for 10 minutes.
4. Mix with vegetables and serve.

LOADED SUMMER BRATWURSTS

Cooking Time: 30 minutes

Serving Size: 2

Calories: 260

Ingredients:

- 8 oz. potatoes
- 2 sweet peppers
- 1 jalapeño
- 1 teaspoon mustard
- 2 tablespoon apple cider vinegar
- 2 Bratwurst Sausages
- 2 hot dog buns
- ¼ cup tomato paste

Method:

1. Cut potatoes and vegetables.

2. Cook potatoes and bratwurst sausages
3. Serve with Salad.

FIESTA ENCHILADA SKILLET

Cooking Time: 30 minutes

Serving Size: 2

Calories: 330

Ingredients:
- 1 onion
- 2 garlic cloves
- 1 zucchini
- 1 cup black beans
- 2 tomatoes
- 1 teaspoon cumin
- 2 corn tortillas
- mozzarella
- 1 avocado

Method:
1. Prepare tortilla and black beans with tomatoes, onions and zucchini.
2. Make corn skillets with mozzarella.
3. Heat for 10 minutes and serve.

MEDITERRANEAN FLATBREADS

Cooking Time: 20 minutes

Serving Size: 2

Calories: 380

Ingredients:
- 2 garlic cloves

- 2 apricots
- 1 cup chickpeas
- 1 lemon
- 2 multigrain flatbreads
- 2 oz. Cashew Cheese

Method:
1. Prepare vegetables and make oregano hummus.
2. Heat until cook.
3. Toast flatbread until crispy.
4. Make the sauce in olive oil.
5. Serve with Salad.

CRISPY BLACK BEAN TACOS

Cooking Time: 40 minutes
Serving Size: 2
Calories: 275

Ingredients:
- 1 mango
- 1 avocado
- 1 lime
- 3 garlic cloves
- 1 jalapeño
- black beans
- 1 teaspoon cumin
- 6 corn tortillas
- 4 oz. cabbage
- 3 tablespoon sour cream

Method:
1. Prepare the mango avocado salsa.
2. Blend the cilantro sauce.

3. Mash the beans.
4. Crisp the tortillas.
5. Toss the cabbage and serve.

PULLED BBQ JACKFRUIT SANDWICHES

Cooking Time: 25 minutes

Serving Size: 2

Calories: 235

Ingredients:
- 2 tablespoon apple cider
- 1 teaspoon sugar
- 1 pack jackfruit
- ¼ cup BBQ sauce
- 2 potato buns
- 2 oz. pickles

Method:
1. Make the creamy coleslaw.
2. Prepare and crisp the jackfruit.
3. Serve with BBQ sauce.

CARROT SOCCA CAKES

Cooking Time: 30 minutes

Serving Size: 2

Calories: 320

Ingredients:
- parsley
- garlic
- ¾ cup bean flour

- 4 carrots
- 1 lemon
- red peppers
- ¼ cup olives
- ¼ cup sliced almonds
- 6 oz. green beans

Method:
1. Make the carrot socca batter.
2. Make aioli and olive relish in a pan.
3. Cook the socca for 10 minutes and toast the nuts.
4. Serve with green beans.

ITALIAN CHOPPED SALADS

Cooking Time: 25 minutes

Serving Size: 2

Calories: 260

Ingredients:
- 1 onion
- 1 cucumber
- 4 tomatoes
- 1 cup chickpeas
- ½ teaspoon smoked paprika
- 2 tablespoon pumpkin and sunflower seeds
- 1 garlic clove
- 1 lettuce

Method:
1. Prepare and Cook the vegetables.
2. Roast the chickpeas until cook and toast nuts.
3. Make the creamy parmesan dressing with lettuce and paprika to serve.

BLACK BEAN AVOCADO MELTS

Cooking Time: 15 minutes

Serving Size: 2

Calories: 430

Ingredients:

- 1 avocado
- 13.4 oz. black beans
- ½ teaspoon chipotle Morita powder
- 4 slices bread
- 2 oz. vegan mozzarella

Method:

1. Prepare the fillings with vegetables.
2. Make and grill sandwiches.
3. Serve with sauce.

SUPER GREEN BREAKFAST SANDWICHES

Cooking Time: 15 minutes

Serving Size: 4

Calories: 400

Ingredients:

- 15.5 oz. Organic Tofu
- ½ teaspoon turmeric
- 6 oz. broccoli
- 1 green bell pepper
- 4 muffins
- ¼ cup vegan basil pesto

Method:

1. Prepare and cook scrambles.
2. Add vegetables and cook for 15 minutes.
3. Make sandwiches with fillings and serve.

FALAFEL

Cooking Time: 35 minutes

Serving Size: 2

Calories: 345

Ingredients:

- 1 onion
- ½ oz. parsley
- 1 garlic clove
- 1 lemon
- 13.4 oz. chickpeas
- 4 radishes
- ½ cup of rice
- 1 tablespoon seasoning
- ½ cup bean flour

Method:

1. Cook the rice and prepare vegetables.
2. Make falafel and pan-fry it for 20 minutes.
3. Serve with sauce.

CAPER DILL BAGELS

Cooking Time: 10 minutes

Serving Size: 4

Calories: 350

Ingredients:

- ¼ oz. dill
- 1 red onion
- 1 tomato
- 2 radishes
- 4 wheat bagels
- ¼ cup vegan cream cheese

- 1 tablespoon bagel spice
- 2 tablespoon capers

Method:
1. Prepare toppings with vegetables.
2. Shape bagels and add toppings.

FIGGIE GRILLED CHEESE SANDWICHES

Cooking Time: 10 minutes

Serving Size: 2

Calories: 380

Ingredients:
- 1 pear
- 2 oz. Cashew Cheese
- 4 slices sourdough bread
- 2 fig spread packets
- 2 tablespoon butter

Method:
1. Build sandwiches and fill with ingredients
2. Grill for 10 minutes and serve.

KOREAN TOFU TACOS

Cooking Time: 25 minutes

Serving Size: 2

Calories: 335

Ingredients:
- 1 garlic clove
- 1 ginger
- 1 tablespoon peanut butter

- 2 tablespoon tamari
- 1 teaspoon sugar
- 1 tablespoon sesame oil
- 7 oz. Baked Tofu
- 3.5 oz. vegan cabbage kimchi
- 8 corn tortillas
- ½ oz. fresh cilantro

Method:
1. Mix the sauce and crispy tofu.
2. Make kimchi slaw and serve.

JACKFRUIT TACOS

Cooking Time: 35 minutes

Serving Size: 2

Calories: 450

Ingredients:
- 4 garlic
- 2 onions
- 2 radishes
- 1 avocado
- 1 lime
- 1½ teaspoon cumin
- 1 pepper
- 8 oz. jackfruit
- 6 white thick corn tortillas

Method:
1. Prepare vegetables and make salsa.
2. Caramelize onion and blend salsa.
3. Crisp jackfruit and serve in tortillas.

RED PEPPER HUMMUS QUESADILLAS

Cooking Time: 30 minutes

Serving Size: 2

Calories: 400

Ingredients:

- ¼ cup quinoa
- ¼ cup olives
- 1 lemon
- 1 cucumber
- parsley
- 13.4 oz. chickpeas
- 1 tablespoon tahini
- 2 tortillas
- spinach

Method:

1. Cut the vegetables and cook quinoa in water until boil.
2. Prepare and cook hummus.
3. Build and cook quesadillas for 15 minutes.
4. Serve with the tortilla.

MOROCCAN CARROT PANCAKES

Cooking Time: 40 minutes

Serving Size: 2

Calories: 450

Ingredients:

- 1 cup bean flour
- 3 carrots
- ¾ teaspoon cumin seeds
- 1 orange
- 1 avocado

- 2 tablespoon capers
- ¼ oz. fresh mint
- ¼ cup cilantro

Method:
1. Heat oven 425°F and whisk the batter with ingredients.
2. Toast the cumin and make pancakes with batter.
3. Cut vegetables for the salad and serve.

PESTO GRILLED CHEESE

Cooking Time: 30 minutes

Serving Size: 2

Calories: 305

Ingredients:
- 1 sweet potato
- 2 teaspoon oregano
- 1 Roma tomato
- 4 sourdough bread
- ¼ cup basil pesto
- ⅓ cup mozzarella
- ⅓ cup cheddar

Method:
1. Roast sweet potatoes and build sandwiches.
2. Cook pester-grilled cheese.
3. Fill sandwiches and serve.

Green Goddess Socca Pizza

Cooking Time: 35 minutes

Serving Size: 2

Calories: 405

Ingredients:
- 1¼ cup bean flour

- 13.4 oz. chickpeas
- 1 tablespoon seasoning
- 6 oz. asparagus
- 1 lemon
- 1 avocado
- ¼ oz. tarragon
- 4 oz. arugula

Method:
1. Make the batter and roast chickpeas.
2. Cook asparagus in a pan for 10 minutes.
3. Blend the tarragon avocado mayo.
4. Prepare and heat crust.
5. Make pizza with toppings.
6. Heat in microwave for 10 minutes and serve.

MUSHROOM SHAWARMA

Cooking Time: 35 minutes
Serving Size: 2
Calories: 255

Ingredients:
- vinegar
- ¾ teaspoon turmeric
- 1 red onion
- 8 oz. mushrooms
- 4 oz. curly kale
- 1 oz. parsley
- 4 oz. red cabbage
- 2 multigrain flatbread

Method:
1. Make the turmeric aioli and Roast the vegetables until cook.

2. Make the kale salad and warm flatbreads.
3. Prepare flatbreads and serve.

CAULIFLOWER SHAWARMA

Cooking Time: 25 minutes

Serving Size: 2

Calories: 490

Ingredients:

- 6 oz. cauliflower florets
- 1 shallot
- 1 lemon
- 1 harissa paste
- 1 tablespoon tahini
- 2 oz. shredded red beets
- 2 multigrain flatbreads

Method:

1. Prepare the vegetables.
2. Roast the cauliflower until tender.
3. Make the aioli, slaw and salad.
4. Roll shawarma and serve.
5.

PESTO STUFFED PEPPERS

Cooking Time: 30 minutes

Serving Size: 2

Calories: 420

Ingredients:

- ½ cup quinoa

- 1 bell pepper
- 4 oz. tomatoes
- 2 oz. olives
- 1 lemon
- 2 oz. arugula
- 2 oz. cheese
- 2 tablespoon vegan basil pesto

Method:
1. Cook the quinoa until tender and roast peppers.
2. Prepare toppings and serve with sauce.

BANH MI. SANDWICHES

Cooking Time: 30 minutes

Serving Size: 2

Calories: 295

Ingredients:
- 1 cucumber
- 1 jalapeño
- 2 carrots
- 7 oz. Tofu
- ¼ oz. cilantro
- ¼ oz. mint
- ¼ cup apple cider
- 1 teaspoon sugar
- 2 ciabatta bread
- 1 tablespoon Roland Sriracha

Method:
1. Prepare and pickle vegetables.
2. Cook vegetables for 15 minutes on low heat.
3. Crisp tofu on low heat and make Sriracha mayo.

4. Make sandwiches and serve.

CRISPY CARROT RAVIOLI

Cooking Time: 45 minutes

Serving Size: 2

Calories: 345

Ingredients:
- 4 carrots
- ¼ cup hazelnuts
- ¼ oz. parsley
- 1 apple
- 1 tablespoon vinegar
- ¼ cup vegan cream cheese
- ½ teaspoon pumpkin pie spice
- 20 dumpling wraps
- 3 tablespoon butter
- 2 oz. arugula

Method:
1. Prepare and cook vegetables.
2. Make carrot fillings and cook.
3. Fill ravioli with carrot and toast nuts.
4. Cook ravioli for 10 minutes and serve.

4.2 Snacks Recipes

SPICY PEACH SALSA

Cooking Time: 5 minutes

Serving Size: 2

Calories: 100

Ingredients:
- 1 red onion
- 2 peaches
- ¼ oz. fresh tarragon
- 2 tablespoon vinegar
- Salt

Method:
1. Cut and mix ingredients to make salsa.

EARLY SPRING PESTO

Cooking Time: 5 minutes

Serving Size: 4

Calories: 200

Ingredients:
- 1 oz. basil and arugula
- ½ cup pine nuts
- ½ cup walnuts
- 1 lemon
- Salt and pepper

Method:
1. Blend all ingredients in a mixer and serve.

SPICY GRAPEFRUIT MARGARITA

Cooking Time: 5 minutes

Serving Size: 2

Calories: 250

Ingredients:

- Salt
- 1 jalapeño
- 2 teaspoon agave
- 2 oz. tequila
- 4 oz. lime juice
- 2 oz. grapefruit juice

Method:

- Blend all ingredients until smooth.

LEMON MERINGUE PIE

Cooking Time: 60 minutes

Serving Size: 4

Calories: 430

Ingredients:

- 2 cups flour
- 1 cup of sugar
- ½ cup cashew milk
- 4 lemons
- 16 oz. silken tofu
- ¾ cup lemon juice
- 5 tablespoons cornstarch
- 1 can beans
- 2 teaspoons cream of tartar
- 2 teaspoons vanilla powder

Method:

1. Prepare the fillings with ingredients and bake crust.
2. Bake pie for 5 to 8 minutes at 460°F.
3. Serve with salad.

CAULIFLOWER BLUEBERRY SMOOTHIE

Cooking Time: 5 minutes

Serving Size: 4

Calories: 330

Ingredients:
- 2 cups blueberries
- ¼ cup almond butter
- ½ cup yoghurt
- ½ teaspoon pumpkin pie spice
- 1 cup almond milk
- 8 oz. cauliflower
- 2 dates

Method:
Blend all ingredients in a mixer and serve.

STUFFED MUSHROOMS

Cooking Time: 35 minutes

Serving Size: 4

Calories: 100

Ingredients:
- 1 lb. cremini mushrooms
- 1 shallot
- Salt and pepper
- 2 oz. spinach

- ½ cup breadcrumbs
- 2 oz. Cashew Cheese

Method:

1. Prepare vegetables and make the stuffing with cooked vegetables.
2. Stuff mushroom and cook until golden brown.
3. Serve with sauce.

MINTED HOT CHOCOLATE

Cooking Time: 10 minutes

Serving Size: 4

Calories: 260

Ingredients:

- 180g vegan chocolate chips
- 6 cups non-dairy milk
- Salt
- ½ teaspoon mint extract

Method:

1. Mix ingredients and heat for 10 minutes.
2. Serve with sandwiches.

SILKY CHOCOLATE MOUSSE

Cooking Time: 45 minutes

Serving Size: 4

Calories: 280

Ingredients:

- 5 oz. dark chocolate
- 16 oz. silken tofu
- 2 tablespoon maple syrup

- 1 teaspoon vanilla extract

Method:
1. Melt chocolate and mix ingredients.
2. Make mousse with paste and serve with toast.

RANCH ROASTED NUTS

Cooking Time: 20 minutes

Serving Size: 4

Calories: 540

Ingredients:
- 3 cups mixed nuts
- 1 teaspoon garlic powder
- 1 teaspoon onion powder
- 1 teaspoon paprika
- 2 tablespoon dill
- Salt

Method:
1. Roast nuts until golden brown.

SALTED ALMOND THUMBPRINT COOKIES

Cooking Time: 60 minutes

Serving Size: 4

Calories: 190

Ingredients:
- 1¼ cup almond flour
- 2 tablespoon maple syrup
- 1 teaspoon vanilla extract
- 3 tablespoon almond butter

- ¼ cup vegan chocolate chips
- Salt

Method:
1. Mix ingredients and prepare the batter.
2. Bake cookies on 350°F for 25 minutes.

MOLASSES CRINKLE COOKIES

Cooking Time: 45 minutes

Serving Size: 4

Calories: 120

Ingredients:
- 2 cups flour
- 2 ½ teaspoon baking soda
- 1 ½ teaspoon cinnamon
- 1 teaspoon ginger
- ½ teaspoon cardamom
- ½ cup vegan butter
- ⅔ cup of sugar
- ½ cup molasses
- 1 teaspoon vanilla extract
- Salt

Method:
1. Prepare the batter and make cookies.
2. Bake on 360°F for 20 minutes.

VEGAN EGGNOG

Cooking Time: 10 minutes

Serving Size: 4

Calories: 560

Ingredients:

- ½ cup cashews
- 28 oz. coconut milk
- ⅓ cup of sugar
- 1 teaspoon vanilla extract
- ½ teaspoon cinnamon
- ¼ teaspoon nutmeg

Method:

1. Soak and blend cashews.
2. Heat and serve.

CHOCOLATE PEANUT BUTTER PIE

Cooking Time: 45 minutes

Serving Size: 4

Calories: 460

Ingredients:

- ¾ cup dates
- 1 cup cashews
- 2 tablespoon cocoa powder
- 1 cup peanut butter
- ½ teaspoon vanilla powder
- ½ cup vegan chocolate chips
- 3 tablespoon peanuts

Method:

1. Make the crust and chocolate.
2. Fill and set the pie for 20 minutes.

MANGO DRINK

Cooking Time: 5 minutes

Serving Size: 4

Calories: 360

Ingredients:

- 2 fresh mangos
- 1 cup dairy-free milk
- ⅛ teaspoon cardamom

Method:

1. Mix ingredients and blend.

PEANUT BUTTER SESAME COOKIES

Cooking Time: 20 minutes

Serving Size: 4

Calories: 150

Ingredients:

- 1 cup peanut butter
- 5 tablespoon maple syrup
- 1 teaspoon sesame seeds
- Salt

Method:

1. Make the dough and bake cookies on 450°F for 20 minutes.

FRESH FRUIT AND COCONUT POPSICLES

Cooking Time: 10 minutes

Serving Size: 4

Calories: 180

Ingredients:

- 2 limes
- 13 oz. coconut milk
- 3 tablespoon agave
- 2 cups fresh mixed berries

Method:

1. Blend all ingredients and freeze.

CLASSIC COLESLAW

Cooking Time: 10 minutes

Serving Size: 4

Calories: 200

Ingredients:

- 12 oz. green cabbage
- 1 carrot
- 1 tablespoon apple cider vinegar

Method:

1. Prepare vegetables and mix.
2. Cook for 10 minutes to make coleslaw.

CRUNCHY WINTER VEGETABLE SALAD

Cooking Time: 15 minutes

Serving Size: 4

Calories: 110

Ingredients:

- 1 fennel bulb
- 1 carrot
- 4 radishes
- 1 radicchio

- ¼ oz. fresh tarragon
- 1 teaspoon mustard
- 1 tablespoon vinegar
- 2 tablespoon pomegranate seeds

Method:
1. Prepare vegetables and mix all ingredients.
2. Add seasoning and make the tarragon vinaigrette.

MATCHA EARTH BITES

Cooking Time: 20 minutes

Serving Size: 4

Calories: 330

Ingredients:
- 2 cups rolled oats
- 1 tablespoon Matcha powder
- ¼ cup maple syrup
- ¼ cup cashew butter
- 1 banana
- ½ cup blueberries

Method:
1. Mix ingredients and roll balls with fillings.
2. Freeze and serve.

CASHEW AND DRIED CHERRY GRANOLA

Cooking Time: 60 minutes

Serving Size: 4

Calories: 320

Ingredients:

- 3 cups rolled oats
- 1 cup almonds
- 1 cup cashews
- ½ cup coconut
- ¼ cup dark brown sugar
- ¼ cup maple syrup
- ½ teaspoon salt
- 1 cup tart cherries

Method:
1. Heat oven at 250°F.
2. Mix ingredients and heat granola in oven for 10 minutes.

MISO POWER DRESSING

Cooking Time: 5 minutes

Serving Size: 4

Calories: 150

Ingredients:
- 2 lemons
- ½ cup hemp seeds
- 2 tablespoon white miso paste
- 1 tablespoon sesame seeds
- Salt

Method:
1. Mix ingredients in a mixer and serve.

BLOOD ORANGE SALAD

Cooking Time: 25 minutes

Serving Size: 4

Calories: 430

Ingredients:

- 8 oz. red beets
- 1 fennel bulb
- 1 lettuce
- 2 oz. radishes
- 2 blood oranges
- 2 teaspoon maple syrup
- 2 tablespoon hazelnuts
- Salt and pepper

Method:

1. Roast the beets on low heat and cut the fennel.
2. Prepare vegetables and orange.
3. Cook vegetables until tender.
4. Mix and serve.

POMEGRANATE SPARKLING SPRITZ

Cooking Time: 5 minutes

Serving Size: 4

Calories: 100

Ingredients:

- 6 oz. chilled prosecco
- 6 oz. chilled pomegranate juice
- 2 teaspoon fresh lemon juice

Method:

1. Prepare, mix and serve the cocktail.
2.

LEEK AND SUN-DRIED TOMATO QUICHE

Cooking Time: 35 minutes

Serving Size: 4

Calories: 330

Ingredients:

- Leek
- ½ cup tomatoes
- ¼ cup basil leaves
- 15 oz. tofu
- ½ teaspoon turmeric
- 1 teaspoon oregano
- 1 vegan premade pie crust

Method:

1. Prepare the vegetables and crisp tofu.
2. Cook the leek for 15 minutes.
3. Blend and bake quiche fillings.
4. Serve with sauce.

MACAO HOT CHOCOLATE

Cooking Time: 10 minutes

Serving Size: 4

Calories: 450

Ingredients:

- 2 tablespoon cacao powder
- 2 tablespoon Macao powder
- ¼ cup maple syrup
- 2 teaspoon vanilla extract
- ½ teaspoon cinnamon
- 3 cups almond milk

- 1 5.5 oz. coconut milk
- ¼ cup powdered sugar

Method:

1. Make hot chocolate and coconut whipped cream.
2. Mix until fluffy and serve.

BUTTERNUT SQUASH BISQUE

Cooking Time: 20 minutes

Serving Size: 4

Calories: 190

Ingredients:

- 1 onion
- 12 oz. butternut squash
- 1 5.5-oz can coconut milk
- 1 orange
- Salt and pepper

Method:

1. Prepare vegetables and cook.
2. Prepare and blend bisque in vegetables to serve.

CLASSIC GRAVY

Cooking Time: 20 minutes

Serving Size: 4

Calories: 60

Ingredients:

- 1 shallot
- 2 tablespoon vegan butter
- 2 teaspoon fresh thyme leaves

- 2 tablespoon flour
- 1 Not-Chick's bouillon cube

Method:
1. Prepare vegetables and make gravy.

GOLDEN BEET AND YUKON MASH

Cooking Time: 25 minutes

Serving Size: 4

Calories: 160

Ingredients:
- 12 oz. golden beets
- 1 lb. Yukon potatoes
- ¼ cup vegan butter
- Salt and pepper

Method:
1. Cook beets and potatoes until smooth.
2. Mash and serve.

PUMPKIN PIE

Cooking Time: 60 minutes

Serving Size: 4

Calories: 260

Ingredients:
- 2 cups flour
- 2 tablespoon sugar
- ¼ teaspoon salt
- 6 tablespoon cashew milk
- 5 tablespoon vegan butter)

- 2 cups pumpkin puree
- 1 teaspoon vanilla
- 3 tablespoon cornstarch
- 2 teaspoon pumpkin pie spice
- ¼ cup brown sugar
- 1 tablespoon maple syrup

Method:
1. Bake the crust and prepare fillings.
2. Bake pie on 250°F for 20 minutes and serve.

HOMEMADE CRANBERRY SAUCE

Cooking Time: 25 minutes

Serving Size: 4

Calories: 130

Ingredients:
- 1 lb. fresh or frozen cranberries
- ½ cup of sugar
- ¼ teaspoon salt

Method:
1. Mix ingredients to make cranberry sauce and serve.

4.3 Salad Recipes

WARM JAPANESE YAM AND SHIITAKE SALAD

Cooking Time: 30 minutes

Serving Size: 2

Calories: 420

Ingredients:
- 1 Japanese yam
- 6 oz. shiitake mushrooms
- ¼ oz. cilantro
- 1 orange
- 1 jalapeño
- 1 lime
- 1 tablespoon sesame oil
- 6 oz. cabbage
- ¼ cup almonds
- ¼ cup spicy peanut sauce

Method:
1. Roast yam and cook Shiitake.
2. Cut vegetables, mix and serve.

SPROUTING BROCCOLI SALADS

Cooking Time: 30 minutes

Serving Size: 2

Calories: 640

Ingredients:
- ¾ cup farro

- 6 oz. broccoli florets
- 6 oz. Brussels sprouts
- 2 oz. olives
- 1 lemon
- ⅓ cup hemp seeds
- 1 tablespoon white miso paste
- ¼ cup sunflower seeds

Method:
1. Cook the farro on low heat and prepare vegetables.
2. Make miso power dressings using ingredients
3. Mix and serve.

CRISPY LEMON TOFU

Cooking Time: 30 minutes
Serving Size: 2
Calories: 520

Ingredients:
- ½ cup lentils
- 10 oz. tofu
- 1 red onion
- 6 oz. curly kale
- 1 lemon
- 2 tablespoon breadcrumbs
- 1 tablespoon white sesame seeds
- 1 tablespoon vegan butter

Method:
1. Cook lentils.
2. Prepare kale, tofu and vegetables.
3. Mix and serve.

AUTUMN CRUNCH SALADS

Cooking Time: 20 minutes

Serving Size: 2

Calories: 580

Ingredients:

- ¼ cup cashews
- 4 oz. grapes
- 1 apple
- 13.4 oz. chickpeas
- ¼ cup walnuts
- 1 lemon
- 1 tablespoon mustard
- 1 tablespoon white miso paste
- 8 oz. shredded kale and Brussels

Method:

1. Prepare and mix vegetables to serve salad.

MEXICAN COBB SALADS

Cooking Time: 30 minutes

Serving Size: 2

Calories: 410

Ingredients:

- 1 sweet potato
- 1 red onion
- 1 teaspoon cumin seeds
- ¼ oz. cilantro
- 1 lime
- 2 corn tortillas
- 13.4 oz. black beans
- 2 radishes

- 1 avocado

Method:

1. Roast vegetables and crisp tortillas.
2. Prepare toppings and serve salad.

CURRIED CHICKPEA SALADS

Cooking Time: 5 minutes

Serving Size: 2

Calories: 550

Ingredients:

- 13.4 oz. chickpeas
- 1 celery stalk
- 4 oz. cherry tomatoes
- 1 onion
- 2 teaspoon curry powder
- ¼ cup raisins
- 2 oz. spinach

Method:

1. Prepare the bowl using all ingredients and cook for 10 minutes.
2. Mix and serve.

GRILLED CAESAR SALAD

Cooking Time: 30 minutes

Serving Size: 2

Calories: 550

Ingredients:

- ½ cup quinoa
- 2 lettuce

- 15.5 oz. Tofu
- 1 shallot
- 2 oz. tomatoes
- 1 tablespoon liquid smoke
- 1 teaspoon agave

Method:
1. Prepare vegetables and cook quinoa.
2. Grill lettuce and cook tofu.
3. Mix and serve.

HARVEST BOWLS

Cooking Time: 30 minutes
Serving Size: 2
Calories: 570

Ingredients:
- 1 sweet potato
- 1 red onion
- 4 oz. cauliflower florets
- ¼ cup apple cider vinegar
- ¼ oz. fresh tarragon
- 1 lemon
- 1 garlic clove
- 1 avocado
- 3 tablespoon sunflower seeds
- 2 tablespoon hemp seeds
- 4 oz. arugula

Method:
1. Roast vegetables.
2. Make the tarragon ranch dressing with remaining ingredients.
3. Prepare avocado and serve.

CHOPPED GREEK SALADS

Cooking Time: 5 minutes

Serving Size: 2

Calories: 270

Ingredients:

- 13.4 oz. cannellini beans
- 6 oz. pre-cooked quinoa
- 1 cucumber
- 1 shallot
- ¼ oz. fresh mint
- 1 lemon

Method:

1. Mix ingredients to prepare bowl and serve.

CRISPY LEMON TOFU

Cooking Time: 30 minutes

Serving Size: 2

Calories: 520

Ingredients:

- ½ cup lentils
- 10 oz. Tofu
- 1 red onion
- 6 oz. curly kale
- ¼ oz. parsley
- 1 lemon
- 2 tablespoon breadcrumbs
- 1 tablespoon white sesame seeds
- 1 tablespoon vegan butter

Method:

1. Cook lentils and prepare vegetables.

2. Crisp tofu and prepare kale and sauce.
3. Finish lentils and serve.

SPANISH-STYLE TOFU

Cooking Time: 30 minutes

Serving Size: 2

Calories: 590

Ingredients:
- 1 garlic clove
- 1 onion
- 6 oz. broccoli
- 15.5 oz. Tofu
- 1 lemon
- ¼ teaspoon smoked paprika
- 2 radishes
- 1 avocado
- 1 teaspoon paella seasoning

Method:
1. Cut vegetables and prepare aioli.
2. Crisp tofu and make avocado radish salad.

ITALIAN CHOPPED SALADS

Cooking Time: 25 minutes

Serving Size: 2

Calories: 520

Ingredients:
- 1 onion

- 1 cucumber
- 4 oz. cherry tomatoes
- 13.4 oz. chickpeas
- ½ teaspoon smoked paprika
- 2 tablespoon pumpkin seeds
- 2 tablespoon sunflower seeds
- ⅓ cup vegan Caesar dressing
- 2 tablespoon vegan parmesan
- 1 lettuce

Method:
1. Prepare vegetables and roast chickpea.
2. Toast the nuts and make the creamy parmesan dressing.

BRASSICA BOWLS

Cooking Time: 25 minutes

Serving Size: 2

Calories: 400

Ingredients:
- 6 oz. broccoli
- 1 tablespoon Italian spice
- 6 oz. kale
- 2 radishes
- 1 lemon
- 13.4 oz. butter beans
- ¼ cup walnuts

Method:
1. Roast broccoli and make the salad.
2. Crisp the butter beans and serve with salad.

THAI-STYLE BROCCOLI SALAD

Cooking Time: 35 minutes

Serving Size: 2

Calories: 440

Ingredients:

- ¾ cup mung beans
- 1 lime
- 3 tablespoon cashew butter
- 1 tablespoon tamari
- 1 tablespoon chili garlic sauce
- 1 cucumber
- 6 oz. broccoli florets
- ¼ oz. fresh mint

Method:

1. Cook the mung beans until tender and prepare sauce.
2. Prepare vegetables and cook broccoli.
3. Mix and serve.

RAINBOW SALADS

Cooking Time: 30 minutes

Serving Size: 2

Calories: 590

Ingredients:

- 1 blood orange
- 1 teaspoon mustard
- 3 tablespoon vinegar
- ½ cup corn kernels
- 2 carrots
- 1 cucumber
- 1 avocado

- 15.5 oz. Firm Tofu
- ¼ cup Bali BBQ sauce
- 2 tablespoon crispy onions

Method:
1. Prepare the blood orange balsamic by mixing oranges and avocado.
2. Cook vegetables and add seasonings.
3. Cook BBQ tofu and toss the salad.

KALE SALADS

Cooking Time: 5 minutes
Serving Size: 2
Calories: 290

Ingredients:
- 1 mango
- 1 cucumber
- ¼ oz. mint
- 1 lime
- ⅓ cup spicy peanut sauce
- 8 oz. kale beet blend
- 2 tablespoon peanuts

Method:
1. Mix ingredients and prepare salads.

THAI MANGO SALADS

Cooking Time: 35 minutes
Serving Size: 2
Calories: 540

Ingredients:

- 15.5 oz. Tofu
- 2 teaspoon coriander
- 1 Japanese yam
- 1 mango
- 2 radishes
- 1 head romaine lettuce
- ¼ cup peanut sauce
- 1 lime
- 1 tablespoon chili garlic sauce

Method:
1. Roast tofu and yam.
2. Cut vegetables and mix to make the salad.

CHOPPED SALAD

Cooking Time: 30 minutes

Serving Size: 2

Calories: 500

Ingredients:
- 6 oz. Brussels sprouts
- 1 tablespoon bagel spice
- 8 oz. tempeh
- 1 tablespoon tamari
- 2 tablespoon maple syrup
- 2 teaspoon liquid smoke
- 6 oz. kale
- 1 carrot
- 2 tablespoon capers

Method:
1. Roast the Brussels sprouts.
2. Crisp tempeh.

3. Prepare vegetables and toss salad.

ROASTED ROOTS SALADS

Cooking Time: 25 minutes

Serving Size: 2

Calories: 590

Ingredients:

- 8 oz. rice
- 2 rainbow carrots
- ¼ cup pumpkin seeds
- 1½ teaspoon agave
- ¼ teaspoon cinnamon
- ¼ teaspoon cayenne pepper
- 1 orange
- 1 lime
- 2 radishes
- 1 lettuce

Method:

1. Cook rice and roast vegetables.
2. Toast the pumpkin seeds and prepare vinaigrette to mix in salad.

CHOPPED SALADS WITH AVOCADO

Cooking Time: 5 minutes

Serving Size: 2

Calories: 660

Ingredients:

- 4 oz. cherry tomatoes
- 1 avocado

- 1 lettuce
- ⅓ cup vegan Ranch
- 1 radish
- 4 oz. multigrain croutons
- 1 shallot

Method:

1. Mix vegetables and prepare the salad.

ROASTED BUTTERNUT & KALE BOWLS

Cooking Time: 30 minutes

Serving Size: 2

Calories: 740

Ingredients:

- ½ cup millet
- 13.4 oz. chickpeas
- 6 oz. cubed butternut squash
- 1 tablespoon French mustard
- ¼ cup walnuts
- 2 oz. Cashew Cheese
- 1 tablespoon white vinegar
- 2 tablespoon apricot preserves
- 4 oz. curly kale

Method:

1. Roast the squash and chickpeas.
2. Cook millet and make cheese balls.
3. Make the apricot vinaigrette with remaining ingredients and serve.

ANTIPASTO SALAD

Cooking Time: 5 minutes

Serving Size: 2

Calories: 210

Ingredients:

- 1 shallot
- 4 oz. red peppers
- 13.75 oz. artichoke hearts
- 1 lettuce
- 2 tablespoon pine nuts
- 1 tablespoon vinegar
- 2 tablespoon vegan parmesan

Method:

1. Mix all ingredients and prepare the salad.

BUFFALO CHICKPEA SALADS

Cooking Time: 5 minutes

Serving Size: 2

Calories: 440

Ingredients:

- 13.4 oz. chickpeas
- 2 tablespoon hot sauce
- 4 oz. grape tomatoes
- 1 celery stalk
- 1 shallot
- 2 lettuce

Method:

1. Mix all items and prepare the salad.

LIME QUINOA SALADS

Cooking Time: 5 minutes

Serving Size: 2

Calories: 270

Ingredients:

- 12 oz. pre-cooked quinoa
- 7 oz. Baked Tofu
- 1 mango
- 1 lime
- 2 teaspoon sesame seeds

Method:

1. Mix ingredients to prepare the salad.

KIDNEY BEAN SALADS

Cooking Time: 5 minutes

Serving Size: 2

Calories: 410

Ingredients:

- 13.4 oz. kidney beans
- 8 oz. rice
- 1 shallot
- ¼ oz. parsley
- 4 oz. roasted red peppers
- 1 tablespoon rice vinegar
- 1 teaspoon agave

Method:

1. Prepare bowl and mix with vegetables.

RAINBOW CRUNCH SALADS

Cooking Time: 30 minutes

Serving Size: 2

Calories: 620

Ingredients:

- 6 oz. Brussels sprouts
- 2 rainbow carrots
- 8 oz. tempeh
- 1 romaine heart
- 1 apple
- ¼ cup BBQ sauce
- 1 teaspoon French mustard and herb blend

Method:

1. Mix tempeh and prepare vegetables.
2. Mix all ingredients and serve.

Chapter 5: Delicious Plant-Based Lunch and Dinner Recipes

This chapter will cover lunch and dinner recipes that are further classified into oil-free, grains, wraps and burgers, soups and bowls recipes. There are many options for you to decide your lunch and dinner menu keeping in mind calories and ingredients available easily.

5.1 Vegan Oil-Free Lunch and Dinner Recipes

CURRIED CHICKPEA SALAD

Cooking Time: 15 minutes

Serving Size: 6

Calories: 239

Ingredients:

- 3 cups chickpeas
- 3 carrots
- 4 green onions
- ½ cup dates
- ½ vegan mayo
- 1 lemon
- 1 tablespoon curry powder
- ¾ teaspoon garlic powder
- Salt

Method:

1. Blend all spices and boil chickpeas.
2. Mash chickpeas and mix with spices.
3. Cook and serve.

CRANBERRY WALNUT VEGAN CHICKEN SALAD

Cooking Time: 15 minutes

Serving Size: 6

Calories: 324

Ingredients:

- 3 cups cooked chickpeas
- 1 cup celery
- ½ cup cranberries
- ½ cup walnuts
- ½ cup scallions
- Salt

Method:

1. Mash chickpeas and assemble spices.
2. Mix and bring to boil.
3. Serve with salad.

GREEK PASTA SALAD

Cooking Time: 20 minutes

Serving Size: 8

Calories: 303

Ingredients:

- 16 oz. pasta
- 10 oz. olives
- 1 can chickpeas
- ½ red onion
- 1 bell pepper
- 1 cucumber
- 10 oz. tomatoes
- 2 lemons
- Salt

Method:

1. Cook pasta and vegetables.
2. Mix spices and heat for 5 minutes until mix properly.

AMERICAN WALNUT MEAT

Cooking Time: 5 minutes

Serving Size: 3

Calories: 264

Ingredients:

- 1 cup walnuts
- 1 cup mushrooms
- 1 tablespoon tamari
- Salt
- ¾ garlic and onion powder

Method:

1. Mix all ingredients and make a paste.
2. Heat in microwave for 15 seconds at 250°F and serve.

ENCHILADA RICE

Cooking Time: 30 minutes

Serving Size: 6

Calories: 309

Ingredients:

- 1 tablespoon olive oil
- 1 onion
- 3 garlic
- 1 green bell pepper
- 1 ½ cups white rice

- 1 can black beans
- 1 can Corn
- 1 can tomatoes
- 1 ½ cups enchilada sauce

Method:
1. Cook vegetables, beans and rice.
2. Add spices and serve.

ITALIAN WALNUT MEAT

Cooking Time: 5 minutes
Serving Size: 3
Calories: 264

Ingredients:
- 1 cup walnuts
- 1 cup mushrooms
- 2 teaspoons Italian seasoning
- ½ teaspoon garlic
- ½ teaspoon onion
- 1 tablespoon tamari
- Salt

Method:
1. Mix all ingredients and make a paste.
2. Heat in microwave for 15 seconds for 300°F and serve.

TOMATILLO SALSA VERDE

Cooking Time: 25 minutes
Serving Size: 6
Calories: 15

Ingredients:

- 2 lbs. tomatillos
- 1 onion
- 2 cloves garlic
- 2 jalapenos
- 2 cups vegetable broth
- ½ cup cilantro

Method:

1. Boil all ingredients and blend until smooth.

VEGAN POZOLE

Cooking Time: 35 minutes

Serving Size: 6

Calories: 287

Ingredients:

- 1 tablespoon olive oil
- 1 onion
- 1 jalapeno
- 1 teaspoon oregano
- 1 can hominy
- 2 cans pinto beans
- 6 tomatillos
- 4 cups vegetable broth

Method:

1. Cook vegetables and add vegetable broth.
2. Add beans and give pressure for 10 minutes.
3. Set aside and serve.

MEXICAN WALNUT MEAT

Cooking Time: 5 minutes

Serving Size: 3

Calories: 264

Ingredients:

- 1 cup walnuts
- 1 cup mushrooms
- 1 tablespoon cumin
- ½ teaspoon garlic
- ¼ teaspoon chipotle
- 1 tablespoon tamari
- Salt

Method:

1. Mix all ingredients and make a paste.
2. Heat in microwave for 15 seconds at 250°F and serve.

EASY LEMON ROSEMARY WHITE BEAN SOUP

Cooking Time: 25 minutes

Serving Size: 6

Calories: 334

Ingredients:

- white beans
- onion
- 3 carrots
- 1 garlic
- vegetable broth ½ teaspoon
- lemon
- salt and pepper

Method:

1. Cut vegetables and boil with beans.

2. Add water and cook until mix.

VEGAN BAKED ZITI

Cooking Time: 50 minutes

Serving Size: 6

Calories: 447

Ingredients:

- 16 oz. pasta ziti
- parsley

Tomato Sauce

- 1 tablespoon olive oil
- 2 cans whole tomatoes
- 1 small onion
- 3 cloves garlic
- Salt

Method:

1. Mix all tomato sauce ingredients and cook.
2. Boil pasta and mix tomato sauce in it.
3. Serve with parsley.

SOBA NOODLE BOWL

Cooking Time: 20 minutes

Serving Size: 3

Calories: 370

Ingredients:

- 1 pack soba noodles
- 1 cup peas
- 1 cup carrots

- 1 cup cucumber
- 1 cup cabbage
- 3 radishes
- 2 scallions

Method:

1. Mix all ingredients and cook noodles.
2. Serve with miso sauce.

VEGAN TOMATO BASIL SOUP

Cooking Time: 30 minutes

Serving Size: 6

Calories: 81

Ingredients:

- 1 large white onion
- 6 cloves garlic
- 2 ½ lbs. tomatoes
- ½ cup basil leaves
- ½ teaspoon oregano
- 2 cups vegetable broth

Method:

1. Cut and fry vegetables.
2. Add other ingredients and spices.
3. Cook until soup is ready.

VEGAN CREAM

Cooking Time: 5 minutes

Serving Size: 2

Calories: 56

Ingredients:

- 1 cup cashews
- 1 ¼ cups water

Method:

1. Soak cashew and blend with water until creamy.

VEGAN CAULIFLOWER SOUP

Cooking Time: 35 minutes

Serving Size: 6

Calories: 152

Ingredients:

- ¼ cup vegan butter
- 1 large onion
- 1 cauliflower
- 5 cups vegetable broth
- 1 cup vegan cream
- 1 lemon

Method:

1. Cook vegetables and bring to boil.
2. Add cream and lemon juice.

THE ULTIMATE VEGETABLE VEGAN LASAGNA

Cooking Time: 60 minutes

Serving Size: 9

Calories: 463

Ingredients:

- 1 tablespoon olive oil
- 1 onion

- 2 carrots
- 1 zucchini
- 8 oz. mushrooms
- ½ teaspoon Italian seasoning
- 1 package spinach
- pasta sauce 3 cups
- 9 lasagna noodles

Method:
1. Cook noodles, pasta and vegetables separately.
2. Add spices and mix.

VEGAN SPINACH ARTICHOKE DIP

Cooking Time: 20 minutes
Serving Size: 10
Calories: 146

Ingredients:
- 1 ½ cups cashews
- 4 tablespoon nutritional yeast
- 2 garlic cloves
- 1 lemon
- 1 ½ cups almond milk
- 14 oz. spinach
- 1 can artichoke hearts

Method:
1. Soak cashew and blend with other spices.
2. Cook vegetables and artichoke hearts for 15 minutes and mix.
3.

VEGAN GOULASH

Cooking Time: 45 minutes

Serving Size: 6

Calories: 333

Ingredients:

- 2 packages tempeh
- 1 onion
- 4 cloves garlic
- 2 green bell peppers
- 1 can tomatoes
- 1 can tomato sauce
- 1 teaspoon mineral salt
- 3 ½ vegetable broth
- 2 cups elbow pasta

Method:

1. Cook vegetables and add pasta.
2. Add other ingredients and seasonings.
3. Cook for 10 minutes until pasta tender.

STUFFED ACORN SQUASH WITH QUINOA

Cooking Time: 40 minutes

Serving Size: 6

Calories: 302

Ingredients:

- 3 acorn squash
- 1 cup quinoa
- 1 teaspoon garlic powder
- sage leaves ¾ teaspoon
- ¼ cup red onion
- 1 can chickpeas

- ½ cup cranberries

Method:
1. Prepare and roast squash.
2. Cook quinoa and stuffing until tender.
3. Mix squash with stuffing and serve.

VEGAN BUTTERNUT SQUASH MAC AND CHEESE

Cooking Time: 30 minutes

Serving Size: 6

Calories: 466

Ingredients:
- 3 cups butternut squash
- 16 oz. pasta
- 1 cup cashews
- 4 tablespoons nutritional yeast
- 2 cloves garlic
- 1 teaspoon onion
- 1 teaspoon smoked paprika
- 1 lemon
- 2 cups water

Method:
1. Cook butternut squash on 400°F.
2. Soak cashew and cook vegetables.
3. Mix all ingredients and bake with cheese on top for 20 minutes.

5.2 Grains Recipes for Lunch and Dinner

CURRIED BLISTERED GREEN BEANS WITH ORANGE RICE

Cooking Time: 30 minutes

Serving Size: 6

Calories: 406

Ingredients:
- 1 tablespoon peanut butter
- 1 tablespoon tamari
- 1 pound green beans,
- 1 cup carrots
- 3 cloves garlic
- 2 cups cooked cauliflower
- 2 cups rice
- 1 teaspoon orange zest
- 1 orange

Method:
1. Stir spices and cook beans.
2. Add vegetables and mix.

STUFFED POBLANO CHILES

Cooking Time: 30 minutes

Serving Size: 4

Calories: 314

Ingredients:
- 4 large Poblano chili peppers
- 2 cups of rice

- 1½ -oz. black beans
- ½ cup of corn
- ½ cup fresh salsa
- ⅓ cup scallions
- ¼ cup cilantro
- 2 tablespoons green olives
- 2 tablespoons pumpkin seeds

Method:
1. Mix all ingredients and bring to boil.
2. Sprinkle pumpkin seeds when ready.

SPICY TOMATO SUSHI ROLLS

Cooking Time: 60 minutes

Serving Size: 4

Calories: 290

Ingredients:
- 1½ cups vegetable broth
- ¾ cup of rice
- 1½ cups butternut squash
- 4 tomatoes
- 1 tablespoon tamari
- 1 tablespoon Sriracha sauce
- 2 teaspoons tahini
- 1 tablespoon maple syrup
- ½ avocado
- 1 cucumber
- 2 carrots
- 4 scallions

Method:
1. Put vegetables broth on heat and add rice to boil.

2. Add vegetables and make tomato sauce.
3. Mix and serve.

SOPES WITH BEANS AND CORN

Cooking Time: 30 minutes

Serving Size: 12

Calories: 289

Ingredients:
- 18 oz. package polenta
- 2 cups corn
- kidney beans 1½ cups
- tomatoes
- 1 avocado
- ¼ cup scallions
- 1 jalapeño

Method:
1. Cut polenta and bake for 20 minutes at 400°F.
2. Cook vegetables, corn and beans.
3. Mix and serve.

QUICK BROWN RICE CONGEE

Cooking Time: 30 minutes

Serving Size: 4

Calories: 62

Ingredients:
- 1 cup of rice
- 14oz. tofu
- 8 oz. cremini mushrooms

- 3 cups vegetable broth
- 3 slices ginger
- 2 cloves garlic
- 2 scallions

Method:
1. Cook rice and bake tofu.
2. Mix vegetables and broth into the rice.
3. Cook until the rice soaked some of the broth and softened.

GREEN BEANS AND POTATOES WITH MUSTARD VINAIGRETTE

Cooking Time: 25 minutes

Serving Size: 9

Calories: 211

Ingredients:
- 2 lb. red potatoes
- 14 oz. whole green beans
- 1 medium red onion
- 6 tablespoons vinegar
- 3 tablespoons mustard
- 2 teaspoons dill weed
- ½ teaspoon garlic powder
- 4 cups bulgur
- ¼ cup pine nuts

Method:
1. Cook potatoes and beans.
2. Add vegetables and spices in the mixture.
3. Cook for 25 minutes and serve.

GRITS AND GREENS

Cooking Time: 30 minutes

Serving Size: 7

Calories: 450

Ingredients:
- vegetable broth
- 4 cloves garlic
- 1½ cups grits
- 1 onion
- 1 red bell pepper
- 14.5-oz. tomatoes
- 15 oz. pinto beans
- ¼ teaspoon smoked paprika
- 16-oz. cut leaf kale

Method:
1. Heat broth and add grits.
2. Add vegetables and bring to boil.
3. Gradually add kale until wilted.

THAI RICE SALAD BOWLS

Cooking Time: 50 minutes

Serving Size: 4

Calories: 138

Ingredients:
- Almond butter-lime dressing
  - 3 tablespoons almond butter
  - 2 tablespoons lime juice
  - 1½ teaspoons tamari
  - 2 cloves garlic
  - 1 teaspoon ginger

- Bowls
  - ¾ cup of rice
  - ¼ cup cilantro
  - 2 8-oz. sweet potatoes
  - 2 cups red cabbage
  - 2 yellow bell peppers
  - ½ cup scallions
  - Sriracha sauce

Method:
1. Prepare almond butter lime dressing with all ingredients.
2. Boil rice and add vegetables for the bowl.
3. Mix and serve.

FORBIDDEN RICE BOWL WITH QUICK-PICKLED CABBAGE

Cooking Time: 60 minutes

Serving Size: 2

Calories: 305

Ingredients:
- 1 cup red cabbage
- 3 tablespoons lemon juice
- ¾ cup black rice
- 1 tablespoon maple syrup
- 1 tablespoon miso paste
- 1 tablespoon tahini
- 2 cups stir-fry vegetables
- ¼ cup green onions

Method:
1. Combine vegetables and fry.
2. Boil rice until tender.
3. Serve with dressings.

FARRO, MUSHROOM, AND LEEK GRATIN

Cooking Time: 60 minutes

Serving Size: 5

Calories: 323

Ingredients:

- ½ cup cashews
- 3 cups vegetable broth
- 1 cup farro
- ½ cup plant milk
- 1 teaspoon mustard
- ½ teaspoon onion powder
- 3 cups mushrooms
- 1 cup leeks
- ½ cup celery
- ½ cup carrot
- 3 cloves garlic
- 2 cups kale
- ⅓ cup crispbread

Method:

1. Soak cashew and boil broth.
2. Blend cashew and other ingredients.
3. Cook and add kale until wilted.

HERBED INSTANT POT RICE PILAF

Cooking Time: 60 minutes

Serving Size: 6

Calories: 203

Ingredients:

- 2 inches stick cinnamon
- 1 teaspoon cumin seeds

- 1 onion
- 1 cup of rice
- ½ cup of corn
- ½ cup peas
- ½ cup red bell pepper
- ½ cup fresh dill
- ¼ cup fresh cilantro
- 2 tablespoons lemon juice

Method:
1. Cook vegetables and mix spices.
2. Boil rice and mix.

MILLET IN COCONUT CURRY

Cooking Time: 30 minutes

Serving Size: 6

Calories: 512

Ingredients:
- ¾ cup millet
- 1 cup leek
- 5 bay leaves
- 2 cloves garlic
- 1 lb. asparagus
- 1 15-oz. can coconut milk
- 1 date
- ⅛ teaspoon black pepper
- 1 tablespoon lime juice
- 2 tablespoons cilantro

Method:
1. Boil water and add spices and millet.
2. Add asparagus and cook for 10 minutes.

3. Add dates and coconut oil and cook more 10 minutes.

EASY TURMERIC EGGPLANT CURRY

Cooking Time: 45 minutes

Serving Size: 4

Calories: 434

Ingredients:
- 1 large eggplant
- ½ red onion
- 2 cloves garlic
- 3 carrots
- 1 cup mushrooms
- 3 tomatoes
- 3 teaspoons turmeric
- 1 teaspoon ginger
- 1 teaspoon red pepper
- 1½ cups lentils
- 1 can coconut milk
- 2⅔ cups vegetable broth
- 2 cups kale

Method:
1. Bake eggplant for 15 minutes in 450°F.
2. Cook lentils, vegetables and coconut oil and stir 10 minutes.
3. Cut eggplant and mix with lentils to serve.

CARIBBEAN RICE

Cooking Time: 60 minutes

Serving Size: 8

Calories: 398

Ingredients:

- 4 cups vegetable broth
- 1 onion
- 1-2 cloves garlic
- 3 cups butternut squash
- 2 teaspoons curry powder
- 1 teaspoon coriander
- ½ teaspoon cumin
- black pepper
- 1 cup of rice
- ½ cup wild rice
- 1 can kidney beans

Method:

1. Cook broth and add spices and vegetables.
2. Prepare squash and add rice and beans and cook.
3. Mix and serve.

COSTA RICAN RICE AND BEANS

Cooking Time: 40 minutes

Serving Size: 2

Calories: 226

Ingredients:

- ½ onion
- 1 red bell pepper
- 2 cloves garlic
- ¼ teaspoon salt

- ½ cup uncooked rice
- ¾ cup black beans
- Hot sauce to taste

Method:
1. Cook vegetables and spices.
2. Boil rice for 20 minutes and mix.

5.3 Wraps and Burgers Recipes

PEACH AND PEPPER TACOS

Cooking Time: 30 minutes

Serving Size: 12

Calories: 330

Ingredients:
- 1 avocado
- ⅓ cup plant milk
- 2 tablespoons lime juice
- ¼ teaspoon hot pepper sauce
- 1 small clove garlic
- 5 tablespoons orange juice
- 1 teaspoon chili powder
- 2 tablespoons basil
- 4 peaches
- 1 Poblano chili pepper
- 1 yellow onion
- 12 corn tortillas

Method:
1. Make avocado crema with avocado and lime juice.
2. Combine fruits and vegetables in a bowl.
3. Cut oranges and put stuffing in tortillas.
4.

JACKFRUIT BARBECUE SANDWICHES WITH BROCCOLI SLAW

Cooking Time: 30 minutes

Serving Size: 6

Calories: 193

Ingredients:

- ½ avocado
- 2 teaspoons lime juice
- 3 cups shredded broccoli slaw
- 1⅓ cups tomato sauce
- 3 dates
- 1½ teaspoons chili powder
- 2 cloves garlic
- ½ teaspoon smoked paprika
- 14-oz. can green jackfruit
- 1 cup cooked farro
- 6 whole-wheat hamburger buns

Method:

1. Make slaw from avocado.
2. Mix jackfruit and farro to heat for 10 minutes.
3. Add other ingredients in a blender and blend until smooth.
4. Fill hamburgers and serve.

ZOODLE ROLLS WITH PESTO SAUCE

Cooking Time: 30 minutes

Serving Size: 8

Calories: 376

Ingredients:

- 16 large lettuce
- 1 zucchini
- 16 brown rice paper wrappers

- 1 red bell pepper
- 1 yellow bell pepper
- 2 cups basil
- ¼ cup pine nuts
- 3 tablespoons lemon juice
- ⅛ teaspoon black pepper

Method:
1. Combine rice paper, lettuce, zucchini, noodles, and peppers.
2. Wrap with fillings and roll to close.

VEGGIE SUMMER ROLLS

Cooking Time: 30 minutes

Serving Size: 12

Calories: 92

Ingredients:
- 1 tablespoon reduced-sodium soy sauce or tamari
- 1 tablespoon lemon juice
- ¼ teaspoon ginger
- 1 clove garlic
- 2 oz. dried brown rice vermicelli noodles
- rice paper wrappers
- 24 sprigs herbs
- 12 6-inch asparagus spears
- ¾ cup beets
- 2 carrots
- 1 kohlrabi
- 1 avocado

Method:
1. Prepare dipping sauce with tamari and lemon juice.
2. Prepare noodles with package directions.

3. Arrange vegetables, noodles and sauce on wraps and fold gently.

CURRIED MILLET SUSHI

Cooking Time: 45 minutes

Serving Size: 4

Calories: 277

Ingredients:
- 1 cup millet
- 1½ teaspoons curry powder
- 1½ teaspoons onion powder
- ¼ cup of rice vinegar
- 2 tablespoons pure maple syrup
- 1½ teaspoons arrowroot powder
- 4 nori sheets
- 1 sweet pepper
- 2 avocados
- 1 cup spinach

Method:
1. Combine millet, garlic and curry powder.
2. Combine other ingredients in millet and stir.
3. Cut vegetables and make rolls with filling.

BUFFALO CAULIFLOWER PITA POCKETS

Cooking Time: 30 minutes

Serving Size: 8

Calories: 437

Ingredients:
- 2 15-oz. cans chickpeas

- 1 tablespoon mustard
- 2 tablespoons hot sauce
- 1 tablespoon tomato paste
- 1 12- to 16-oz. cauliflower
- ½ cup onion and carrot
- 3 cloves garlic, minced
- 8 lettuce leaves
- 4 pita bread
- ½ cup celery

Method:
1. Mash beans and mix liquid ingredients.
2. Cook vegetables in spices except for lettuce.
3. Place one lettuce and fillings in each pita bread.

TORTILLA ROLL-UPS WITH LENTILS AND SPINACH

Cooking Time: 20 minutes
Serving Size: 15
Calories: 318

Ingredients:
- ½ onion
- 6 small cloves garlic
- 1 15-ounce can lentils
- 1 tablespoon lemon juice
- 3 8-inch tortillas
- 2 cups spinach
- 1 cup oil-free hummus

Method:
1. Sauté onion, garlic and cook lentils in lemon juice for 10 minutes.
2. Wrap tortillas and heat in the microwave for 30 seconds.
3. Assemble other ingredients and wrap to make rolls.

FIVE-INGREDIENT VEGGIE BURGER

Cooking Time: 55 minutes

Serving Size: 4

Calories: 177

Ingredients:

- 2 cups black beans
- 1 onion
- ½ cup quick-cooking rolled oats
- 2 teaspoon chili powder
- 4 hamburger buns
- 4 leaves lettuce
- 1 tomato
- 2 red onion slices

Method:

1. Prepare patties beans, oats and onion.
2. Prepare toppings and make burgers.

SLOPPY JOE PITAS

Cooking Time: 30 minutes

Serving Size: 6

Calories: 307

Ingredients:

- 1 cup bulgur
- 1 onion
- ½ cup green bell pepper
- ½ cup celery
- 2 cloves garlic
- 1¾ cups barbecue sauce
- black pepper
- 3 whole-grain pita bread

Method:

1. Boil bulgur and cook other vegetables.
2. Add sauces and fill pita bread.

STREET CORN TOSTADAS

Cooking Time: 30 minutes

Serving Size: 8

Calories: 760

Ingredients:

- 8 6-inch corn tortillas
- ½ cup onion
- 1 fresh jalapeño
- 3 cloves garlic
- 1 16-oz. package corn
- 1 15-oz. can chickpeas
- ¼ cup plant milk
- 1 tablespoon lime juice

Method:

1. Prepare corn and crisp tortillas in the oven at 250°F.
2. Prepare vegetables and mash chickpeas.
3. Put corn mixture in crisp tortillas.

RAINBOW VEGGIE SLAW WRAP

Cooking Time: 20 minutes

Serving Size: 8

Calories: 223

Ingredients:

- 1 15-oz. can chickpeas

- 3 cups zucchini
- ½ cup carrot
- ½ cup radishes
- ½ cup pea pods
- ½ cup red onion
- ¼ cup fresh dill
- 2 tablespoons white miso paste
- 1½ teaspoons yellow mustard
- 8 - 8-inch tortillas
- 16 lettuce leaves

Method:
1. Mash chickpeas and add seasoning.
2. Prepare tortillas with toppings and add fillings.

FULL-ON TACO BAR

Cooking Time: 30 minutes

Serving Size: 12

Calories: 430

Ingredients:
- 2 large sweet onions
- 1 red bell pepper
- ½ fresh jalapeño pepper
- 2 cloves garlic
- 3 cups lentils
- 1 can refried beans
- 1 cup vegetable stock
- 12, 6-inch corn tortillas

Method:
1. Stir in the lentils, beans, and taco seasoning mix.
2. Cook vegetables and serve vegetable mix lentils with tortillas.

SUPER SLOPPY JOES

Cooking Time: 30 minutes

Serving Size: 6

Calories: 248

Ingredients:

- ⅓ cup dates
- ½ cup yellow onion
- ½ cup celery
- ½ cup green bell pepper
- 2 cloves garlic
- 2 cups cooked wheat berries
- ¼ cup ketchup
- 1 tablespoon tamari sauce
- 6 whole-grain hamburger buns

Method:

1. Combine ingredients and stir for 6 to 7 minutes.
2. Add seasoning and serve.

DEVILED POTATO SANDWICHES

Cooking Time: 30 minutes

Serving Size: 8

Calories: 216

Ingredients:

- 1 large potato
- ½ cup plant milk
- ¼ teaspoon yellow mustard
- 1 celery stalk
- 1 scallion
- 18 slices bread

Method:

1. Boil potato and blend with other ingredients.
2. Make sandwiches with mixture and lettuce leaves.

PLT (GREEN PEA, LETTUCE AND TOMATO) SANDWICH

Cooking Time: 20 minutes

Serving Size: 4

Calories: 152

Ingredients:
- 2½ cups green peas
- ¼ cup basil
- 1 tablespoon nutritional yeast
- 1 tablespoon lemon juice
- 2 garlic cloves
- ½ teaspoon salt
- 1–2 tablespoons water

Method:
1. Add vegetables and boiled peas in a blender.
2. Blend until reach desired consistency and make sandwiches.

5.4 Soups and Bowls Recipes

STRAWBERRY GAZPACHO

Cooking Time: 20 minutes

Serving Size: 5

Calories: 130

Ingredients:
- 1 lb. strawberries
- 1 cucumber
- 1 tomato
- 1 bell pepper
- ½ onion
- 2 cloves garlic
- 1 tablespoon lemon juice
- ¼ to ½ cup vegetable broth

Method:
1. Blend all ingredients and add seasoning.

CHAYOTE SOUP WITH ROASTED HOMINY

Cooking Time: 35 minutes

Serving Size: 7

Calories: 177

Ingredients:
- 1 25-oz. can hominy
- ¼ cup lime juice
- 2 teaspoons arrowroot powder
- 2 teaspoons chilli powder

- ½ teaspoon cumin
- ⅛ teaspoon chipotle
- 2 carrots
- 6 cloves garlic
- 1 teaspoon Mexican oregano
- 2 lb. chayote squash
- 2 cups potatoes
- 2 cups plant milk

Method:
1. Roast hominy and cook potatoes until tender.
2. Mix all ingredients and blend until smooth.

GARLICKY BOK CHOY NOODLE SOUP

Cooking Time: 35 minutes

Serving Size: 11

Calories: 647

Ingredients:
- 4 cups vegetable broth
- 4 cloves garlic
- 1 tablespoon fresh ginger
- 2 teaspoons soy sauce
- 6 ounces of Thai noodles
- 12 carrots
- 3 ounces tofu
- 2 bok
- 12 asparagus
- 1 cup shiitake mushrooms
- 4 scallions

Method:
1. Boil all ingredients until smooth.

2. Serve with lime wedges.

PUMPKIN AND RED LENTIL DAL

Cooking Time: 35 minutes

Serving Size: 4

Calories: 222

Ingredients:

- ½ teaspoon mustard seeds
- 1 teaspoon cumin seeds
- 1 cup onion
- 1 jalapeño chilli
- 1 tablespoon fresh ginger
- 1 small pumpkin
- 1 cup dry red lentils
- 1 cup tomato
- ½ teaspoon turmeric
- ½ teaspoon paprika
- 2 tablespoons lime juice

Method:

1. Boil all ingredients until fully cooked.
2. Add seasonings and serve.

THAI VEGETABLE NOODLE SOUP

Cooking Time: 25 minutes

Serving Size: 6

Calories: 178

Ingredients:

- ½ cup scallions

- 2 tablespoons Thai Spice Blend
- 4 cups vegetable stock
- 1 cup green beans
- 1 cup carrots
- 4 oz. noodles
- 1 cup peas
- 1 cup broccoli
- 1 baby bok choy
- 1 cup plant milk
- 3 tablespoons lime juice
- ⅛ teaspoon of sea salt
- 6 fresh basil leaves

Method:
1. Cook all ingredients until tender and serve.

CREAMY CARROT SOUP

Cooking Time: 40 minutes

Serving Size: 6

Calories: 113

Ingredients:
- ¼ cup cashews
- 1 onion
- 1½ carrots
- 1 red bell pepper
- 1 rosemary
- 4 cloves garlic
- 1 tablespoon lemon juice
- ½ cup fresh pomegranate seeds
- 2 tablespoons parsley

Method:

1. Soak cashew and sauté vegetables.
2. Blend all ingredients and add seasoning

HARVEST VEGETABLE INSTANT POT MINESTRONE

Cooking Time: 30 minutes

Serving Size: 7

Calories: 269

Ingredients:

- 2 cups onions
- 1 cup white beans
- 4 cloves garlic
- 1 cup carrots
- 1 cup celery
- 1 cup parsnips
- 1 cup turnip
- 1 teaspoon basil
- ½ teaspoon thyme
- ½ teaspoon rosemary
- ¼ teaspoon oregano
- 3 cups shell pasta

Method:

1. Give pressure to beans, garlic and onion for 20 minutes.
2. Make tomato sauce and pasta.
3. Mix and serve.

ZUCCHINI, CORN, AND BLACK BEAN SOUP

Cooking Time: 40 minutes

Serving Size: 8

Calories: 243

Ingredients:

- 1 32-oz. almond milk
- 2 cups potatoes
- ½ cup onion
- ½ cup celery
- 2 cloves garlic
- 2 cups Corn
- 1 15-oz. can black beans
- 1 zucchini
- 1 teaspoon thyme
- 2 tablespoons vinegar

Method:

1. Boil potatoes.
2. Mix other ingredients and return to boil.
3. Serve with salad.

CHIPOTLE-WATERMELON GAZPACHO

Cooking Time: 30 minutes

Serving Size: 5

Calories: 116

Ingredients:

- 3 cups watermelon
- ½ cup cilantro
- 1 tablespoon lime juice
- 2 cloves garlic
- ½ teaspoon cumin
- ¼ teaspoon chipotle
- 3 cups tomatoes
- 1 cup cucumber

- ¼ cup red onion

Method:
1. Mix all ingredients and blend until smooth.
2. Freeze for 2 hours before serving.

30-MINUTE CHILI

Cooking Time: 30 minutes

Serving Size: 7

Calories: 101

Ingredients:
- 2 yellow onions
- 1 green bell pepper
- 3 tablespoons chili powder
- 1 tablespoon oregano
- 2 teaspoons cumin
- 4 cloves garlic
- 2, 15-oz. cans pinto beans
- 1, 28-oz. can tomatoes
- 2 cups vegetable broth

Method:
1. Mix all ingredients and boil.
2. Stir until thick and add seasoning.

GARDEN TOMATO SOUP WITH CHICKPEAS

Cooking Time: 40 minutes

Serving Size: 7

Calories: 123

Ingredients:

- 3 lb. tomatoes
- 1 cup sweet onion
- 1 cup red bell pepper
- 1 15-oz. can chickpeas
- 1 cup vegetable broth
- 1 cup grape tomatoes
- ¼ cup raw pumpkin seeds

Method:
1. Boil chickpea and broth.
2. Blend other ingredients and add into boiling mixture.
3. Stir until thick and smooth.

MEDITERRANEAN LENTIL AND SPINACH SOUP

Cooking Time: 60 minutes

Serving Size: 9

Calories: 175

Ingredients:
- 32 ounces vegetable broth
- 1 cup green lentils
- 1 onion
- 2 stalks celery
- 1 carrot
- 1 green zucchini
- 1 teaspoon cumin
- 1 teaspoon oregano
- 2 tomatoes
- 4 cups spinach

Method:
1. Boil all ingredients except tomatoes and squash.
2. Add squash and tomatoes gradually.

3. Whisk until mixture smooth.

RED CURRY NOODLE SOUP

Cooking Time: 40 minutes

Serving Size: 8

Calories: 290

Ingredients:

- 2 tablespoons curry paste
- 6 cloves garlic
- 2 tablespoon ginger
- 1 red bell pepper
- 1 cup pea pods
- 2 carrots
- 2 cups coconut milk
- ¼ cup basil leaves
- ¼ cup cilantro leaves
- ½ onion
- 1 jalapeño,

Method:

1. Cook noodles and boil other ingredients.
2. Add cooked noodles in mixture and heat.

CREAMY WILD RICE SOUP

Cooking Time: 60 minutes

Serving Size: 6

Calories: 292

Ingredients:

- ½ cup leek

- 5 cloves garlic
- red bell pepper
- ½ cup carrot
- ¾ cup wild rice
- 1 package button mushrooms
- 4 cups vegetable stock
- 1 cup almond flour
- 1 cup chickpea flour

Method:
1. Boil ingredients and add rice until tender.
2. Mix almond flour and chickpea flour in boiled rice.
3. Stir continuously and add water to reach desire consistency.

ZESTY WHITE BEAN CHILI

Cooking Time: 55 minutes

Serving Size: 10

Calories: 245

Ingredients:
- 3 bell peppers
- 1 onion
- 3 celery stalks
- 2 carrots
- 12 cloves garlic
- 2 teaspoons cumin
- 2 teaspoons oregano
- 2 tomatoes
- 2 tablespoons chili powder
- 2 tablespoons paprika
- 3 cans cannellini beans
- 1 cup Corn

- 1 tablespoon lemon juice
- ¼ cup cilantro

Method:
1. Boil all ingredients except beans, vinegar and corn.
2. Add beans, corn and vinegar when the mixture starts boiling.
3. Stir continuously and serve with sprinkled cilantro.

Chapter 6: Plant-Based Sweets and Side Dishes

This chapter will cover sweet dishes, desserts and side dishes based on plants and easy to cook with limited ingredients.

6.1 Desserts and Sweets

MANGO MOUSSE

Cooking Time: 60 minutes

Serving Size: 4

Calories: 480

Ingredients:

- 3 mangoes
- 13.5 oz. coconut cream
- 1 tablespoon agave
- Salt

Method:

1. Blend all ingredients and make the mousse.

LOW CARB COOKIE BARS

Cooking Time: 20

Serving Size: 6

Calories: 330

Ingredients:

- 1½ cup vegan chocolate chips

- 1½ cup peanut butter
- Salt
- 1 cup almond flour
- 4 tablespoon agave

Method:
1. Mix ingredients to make bars and prepare toppings.

TAHINI CHOCOLATE CHIP COOKIES

Cooking Time: 50 minutes

Serving Size: 24

Calories: 200

Ingredients:
- ½ cup of coconut oil
- ½ cup tahini
- ⅓ cup of sugar
- ⅓ cup of cane sugar
- ½ cup non-dairy milk
- 1 teaspoon vanilla extract
- 1 ¼ cups all-purpose flour
- 2 tablespoon cornstarch
- ½ teaspoon baking powder
- ½ teaspoon baking soda
- 1 ½ cup vegan chocolate chips

Method:
1. Mix wet and dry ingredients separately.
2. Whisk both mixtures and prepare cookies.
3. Bake at 250°F for 30 minutes.

VEGAN LEMON BARS

Cooking Time: 60 minutes

Serving Size: 8

Calories: 500

Ingredients:

- 1 cup raw cashews
- ¾ cup oat flour
- ¾ cup almond flour
- 5 tablespoon coconut oil
- 1 cup coconut cream
- ½ cup lemon juice
- 2 tablespoon cornstarch
- ¼ cup maple syrup

Method:

1. Make and bake the crust.
2. Make the fillings and bake the bars for 20 minutes at 350°F.

PEANUT BUTTER AND BERRY BITES

Cooking Time: 20 minutes

Serving Size: 20

Calories: 100

Ingredients:

- ¾ cup rolled oats
- ¾ cup peanut butter
- 8 dates
- 1 tablespoon cacao nibs
- ¼ cup shredded coconut
- ½ cup peanuts
- 6 blackberries or strawberries

Method:

1. Prepare and mix the ingredients to make the bites.

MACERATED BERRIES

Cooking Time: 30 minutes

Serving Size: 4

Calories: 100

Ingredients:
- 2 cups mixed berries
- ¼ cup granulated sugar
- 13.5 oz. coconut cream
- ¼ cup powdered sugar

Method:
1. Macerate the berries and whip the coconut cream.
2. Prepare other toppings and serve.

LEMON MERINGUE PIE

Cooking Time: 60 minutes

Serving Size: 4

Calories: 150

Ingredients:
- 1 tablespoon coconut oil
- 2 cups flour
- ½ cup cashew milk
- 5 tablespoon vegan butter
- 4 lemons
- 16 oz. silken tofu
- ¾ cup lemon juice
- 5 tablespoon cornstarch

- 2 teaspoon vanilla powder

Method:
1. Bake the crust and make the meringue.
2. Make filling and bake the pie.

SILKY CHOCOLATE MOUSSE

Cooking Time: 45 minutes

Serving Size: 4

Calories: 280

Ingredients:
- 5 oz. cocoa dark chocolate
- 16 oz. silken tofu
- 2 tablespoon maple syrup
- 1 teaspoon vanilla extract

Method:
1. Blend the chocolate and make the mousse.

MOLASSES CRINKLE COOKIES

Cooking Time: 45 minutes

Serving Size: 4

Calories: 120

Ingredients:
- 2 cups all-purpose flour
- 2 ½ teaspoon baking soda
- 1 teaspoon ginger
- ½ teaspoon cardamom
- ½ cup vegan butter
- ⅔ cup of sugar

- ½ cup blackstrap molasses
- 2 tablespoon sugar

Method:
1. Mix dry and wet ingredients separately.
2. Mix all mixtures and make cookies.
3. Bake for 30 minutes at 400°F.

ROSEMARY AND SEA SALT CHOCOLATE CHIP COOKIES

Cooking Time: 25 minutes

Serving Size: 2

Calories: 350

Ingredients:
- 2 tablespoon flaxseed meal
- ¾ cup of coconut oil
- 2 sprigs fresh rosemary
- 2 cups all-purpose flour
- 1 teaspoon baking powder
- ¾ teaspoon baking soda
- ½ cup of sugar
- ¾ cup vegan chocolate chips

Method:
1. Make the flax egg and infuse coconut oil.
2. Make cookie dough and bake at 400°F.

BIRTHDAY CAKE PROTEIN BALLS

Cooking Time: 20 minutes

Serving Size: 4

Calories: 120

Ingredients:
- ½ cup rolled oats
- 2 tablespoon pea protein
- ¾ cup coconut flakes
- 2 teaspoon vanilla powder
- ¼ cup creamy cashew butter
- ¼ cup macadamia nuts
- ¼ cup agave
- ½ cup rainbow sprinkles

Method:
1. Blend the ingredients and make balls.

COCONUT PEANUT BUTTER BITES

Cooking Time: 60 minutes

Serving Size: 4

Calories: 160

Ingredients:
- 1 cup dates
- ¾ cup peanut butter
- 1 tablespoon coconut oil
- 1 cup coconut
- 1 teaspoon vanilla extract
- 1 tablespoon agave syrup

Method:
1. Soak the dates and blend with other ingredients.
2. Make the dough and bake bites at 250°F for 30 minutes.

LEMON COCONUT BARS

Cooking Time: 10 minutes

Serving Size: 4

Calories: 156

Ingredients:

- 1 ½ cup coconut
- 1 cup rolled oats
- ½ cup oat flour
- 1 lemon
- 5 tablespoons agave
- 2 tablespoons coconut oil
- 1 teaspoon vanilla

Method:

1. Blend ingredients and make the dough.
2. Cut into bars and bake on 370°F for 20 minutes.

VANILLA NICE-CREAM

Cooking Time: 5 minutes

Serving Size: 4

Calories: 60

Ingredients:

- 2 bananas
- 2 teaspoon vanilla extract
- Nut milk or water

Method:

1. Blend all ingredients and add flavors.
2. Freeze for 2 hours.

GRILLED PEACHES

Cooking Time: 20 minutes

Serving Size: 4

Calories: 540

Ingredients:

- 2 fresh peaches
- 2 tablespoon agave
- 1 can coconut cream
- 1 teaspoon vanilla extract
- 1 tablespoon coconut sugar
- 1 tablespoon coconut or vegetable oil

Method:

1. Prepare and grill the peaches.
2. Whip coconut cream and serve.

CINNAMON SUGAR PITA CHIPS

Cooking Time: 15 minutes

Serving Size: 4

Calories: 180

Ingredients:

- 2 pitas
- 1 tablespoon coconut oil
- 1 tablespoon cane sugar
- 2 teaspoon cinnamon
- 1 ripe peach
- 1 tablespoon red onion
- 1 tablespoon vinegar

Method:

1. Toast the pita chips and prepare salsa to serve.

CHOCOLATE COVERED BANANAS

Cooking Time: 30 minutes

Serving Size: 4

Calories: 320

Ingredients:

- 7 ripe bananas
- 14 popsicle sticks
- 2 cups dark chocolate chips
- 2 tablespoon coconut oil
- ¼ cup creamy cashew butter
- ¼ cup coconut
- ¼ cup hemp seeds
- ¼ cup raw sliced almonds
- ¼ cup dried blueberries

Method:

1. Prepare banana and melt chocolate.
2. Dip banana in chocolate and freeze.

STRAWBERRY RHUBARB PIE

Cooking Time: 60 minutes

Serving Size: 4

Calories: 350

Ingredients:

- 3 cups strawberries
- 2 cups rhubarb lattice
- 1 lime
- ½ cup of cane sugar
- 1½ teaspoon salt
- 2¼ cup all-purpose flour
- 1 tablespoon vanilla powder

- ½ cup of coconut oil
- 1 cup maple syrup

Method:

1. Marinate fruits and build dough.
2. Make and fill the pie.
3. Create a lattice crust and make toppings.

TAMARIND MANGO SMOOTHIE

Cooking Time: 5 minutes

Serving Size: 4

Calories: 200

Ingredients:

- 1 fresh mango
- 1 lemon
- 1 tablespoon tamarind paste
- 1 can coconut milk

Method:

1. Chop mangoes and blend all ingredients until smooth.

CHERRY CHIA PUDDING

Cooking Time: 40 minutes

Serving Size: 4

Calories: 430

Ingredients:

- ½ cup cashew milk
- 1 teaspoon vanilla extract
- 2 tablespoon agave
- ⅓ cup cherry preserves

- ⅓ cup chia seeds
- 1 banana
- 1 kiwi
- 3 oz. cherries
- 1 tablespoon hemp seeds

Method:
1. Mix all ingredients and make pudding.

CHOCOLATE-DIPPED SPICED APRICOTS

Cooking Time: 10 minutes

Serving Size: 2

Calories: 170

Ingredients:
- 8 oz. apricots
- 2 oz. vegan chocolate chips
- ¼ teaspoon cayenne pepper
- ¼ teaspoon cinnamon

Method:
1. Melt the chocolate and dip fruit.
2. Freeze for 1 hour.

CASHEW BUTTER POWER BITES

Cooking Time: 15 minutes

Serving Size: 2

Calories: 120

Ingredients:
- ½ cup chocolate protein powder

- ¼ cup creamy cashew butter
- ¼ cup brown rice syrup
- ¼ cup chia seeds

Method:
1. Mix all ingredients and make bites.

PISTACHIO DATE BALLS

Cooking Time: 15 minutes

Serving Size: 2

Calories: 220

Ingredients:
- 1 cup dates
- ½ cup pistachios
- 2 tablespoon coconut

Method:
1. Blend all ingredients and roll to make balls.

PEANUT BRITTLE

Cooking Time: 25 minutes

Serving Size: 2

Calories: 290

Ingredients:
- ½ cup peanut halves
- ½ cup vegan butter
- ¾ cup of sugar
- 1 teaspoon vanilla extract

Method:
1. Toast the nuts.

2. Make caramel and pour on toasts.

TROPICAL PROTEIN SHAKE

Cooking Time: 10 minutes

Serving Size: 2

Calories: 190

Ingredients:
- 8 oz. pineapple chunks
- 3 oz. cherries
- 4 oz. mango
- 1 scoop pea protein
- ¼ cup of orange juice
- 1 tablespoon agave

Method:
1. Blend all ingredients until smooth.

PEANUT BUTTER BANANA OAT BALLS

Cooking Time: 55 minutes

Serving Size: 2

Calories: 137

Ingredients:
- 3 ripe bananas
- 3 cups oats
- ½ cup peanut butter
- 2 tablespoon maple syrup
- 1 tablespoon vanilla
- ⅓ cup of chocolate chips

Method:

1. Mash bananas and make the dough.
2. Add chocolate chip and roll the dough to make balls.

SUPERFOOD SNACK BARS

Cooking Time: 20 minutes

Serving Size: 2

Calories: 190

Ingredients:
- 6 oz. dates
- 2 oz. blueberries
- 4 tablespoon almond butter
- 3 tablespoon coconut oil
- ¾ cup sunflower seeds
- ¾ cup shredded coconut
- 5 oz. vegan dark chocolate

Method:
1. Form the bars and microwave at 400°F until crispy.

CHAI TEA LATTE

Cooking Time: 10 minutes

Serving Size: 2

Calories: 35

Ingredients:
- 2-4 cinnamon sticks
- 4-8 cloves
- 4 black peppercorns
- 1 teaspoon ground nutmeg
- 1 tablespoon loose leaf black tea

- 1 cup almond milk
- 2 tablespoon agave
- 2 teaspoon vanilla extract

Method:
1. Prepare and steep tea.
2. Add vanilla milk and serve.

6.2 Side Dishes

CREAMY COCONUT CARROT SOUP

Cooking Time: 25 minutes

Serving Size: 2

Calories: 100

Ingredients:
- 1 pound carrots
- 1 onion
- 2 cups vegetable stock
- 1 can coconut milk
- ¼ cup cilantro leaves
- 2 avocados
- 1 lime

Method:
1. Cut all vegetables and fry in olive oil.
2. Toast quinoa and blend vegetables until mix.
3. Cut avocado and garnish.

WINTER CHOWDER

Cooking Time: 30 minutes

Serving Size: 2

Calories: 450

Ingredients:
- 1 onion
- 6 oz. cauliflower
- 2 tablespoon vegan sour cream
- 2 teaspoon radish

- 8 oz. root vegetable
- 2 teaspoon mustard and herb blend
- 2 teaspoon concentrated vegetable broth
- 1 ancient grain roll

Method:
1. Prepare vegetables and cook.
2. Start chowder to boil vegetables.
3. Make garlic toast and serve.

GRILLED CORN AND CHERRY TOMATO SALSA

Cooking Time: 12 minutes

Serving Size: 4

Calories: 140

Ingredients:
- 2 corn
- 1 tomato
- ¼ cup cilantro leaves
- 1 shallot

Method:
1. Grill the corn and prepare vegetables.
2. Toss the salsa and serve.

CORNMEAL AREPAS

Cooking Time: 35 minutes

Serving Size: 2

Calories: 440

Ingredients:
- 2 tablespoon flour

- 2 tablespoon vegan butter
- 1 tablespoon sugar
- 1 orange
- 1 onion
- 1 zucchini
- 2 oz. radish
- 1 lime
- 1 can black beans

Method:
1. Mix ingredients to make the dough.
2. Prepare salsa and make Arepas.

SPICY ALMOND BUTTER ODON

Cooking Time: 35 minutes

Serving Size: 2

Calories: 400

Ingredients:
- 7 oz. Brussels sprouts
- 4 oz. carrot
- 2 scallions
- 7 oz. udon noodles
- 1 lime
- 1 garlic clove
- 3 tablespoon almond butter
- 2 tablespoon tamari
- 1 tablespoon chili garlic sauce
- 2 teaspoon maple syrup

Method:
1. Cook vegetables and make almond butter sauce.
2. Make Brussels and sauce.

3. Cook udon noodles and serve.

SWEET POTATO CHAT

Cooking Time: 35 minutes

Serving Size: 2

Calories: 450

Ingredients:
- 1 sweet potato
- ¾ cup split mung beans
- 1 onion
- Fresh cilantro
- 1 pepper
- 3 tablespoon vegan yoghurt
- 1 lime
- 1 teaspoon tamarind paste
- ½ cup of rice
- 2 oz. spinach

Method:
1. Boil sweet potato and cook mung beans.
2. Prepare vegetables and mix masala yoghurt.

OKONOMIYAKI

Cooking Time: 35 minutes

Serving Size: 2

Calories: 360

Ingredients:
- 1½ teaspoon starch
- 8 oz. sweet potato

- 1¼ cups cabbage
- ½ cup all-purpose flour
- ½ cup brown rice flour
- 2 oz. noodles
- 2 scallions
- Fresh ginger
- 1 teaspoon rice vinegar
- 1 tablespoon sweet soy

Method:

1. Prepare batter and vegetables.
2. Make noodles and add batter veggies and sauces.
3. Mix and enjoy okonomiyaki.

SOUTHERN SPOONBREAD

Cooking Time: 40

Serving Size: 2

Calories: 710

Ingredients:

- ½ cup almond milk
- 1 ½ teaspoon maple syrup
- ½ cup cornmeal
- ¼ teaspoon baking soda
- 1 ¼ teaspoon baking powder
- 1 shallot
- 1 tomato
- 2 tablespoon vegan butter
- 1 tablespoon tomato paste
- 1 cup peas

Method:

1. Prepare spoon bread and vegetables.

2. Make the batter and tomato gravy.
3. Mix and serve.

TEMPURA SWEET POTATO BAO

Cooking Time: 30 minutes

Serving Size: 2

Calories: 730

Ingredients:
- 1 sweet potato
- ½ cup flour
- 1 peach
- ½ cup Kimchi
- 1 scallion
- 1 lemon
- ¼ cup vegan mayonnaise
- 6 bao buns

Method:
1. Prepare sweet potatoes and mix kimchi.
2. Build bao and add fillings to serve.

SWEET CORN RISOTTO

Cooking Time: 45 minutes

Serving Size: 2

Calories: 650

Ingredients:
- 1 onion
- 1 ear of corn
- ¾ cup of rice

- 1 lemon
- 6 oz. broccoli
- 2 tablespoon vegan parmesan
- 1 tablespoon vegan butter

Method:
1. Sauté the onion and boil rice.
2. Roast broccoli and add corn.
3. Mix and serve.

SPRING RADISH FATTOUSH

Cooking Time: 40

Serving Size: 2

Calories: 500

Ingredients:
- ½ cup of rice
- 1 fennel bulb
- 4 oz. tomatoes
- 1 Persian cucumber
- 2 scallions
- 1 pita
- 5 oz. egg radishes
- 1 lemon
- 6 oz. chopped romaine

Method:
1. Cook rice and prepare fennel.
2. Slice vegetables and mix ingredients and spices.

CRISPY TURNIP CAKES

Cooking Time: 40 minutes

Serving Size: 2

Calories: 410

Ingredients:

- ¾ cup white quinoa
- 1 tablespoon flax meal
- 2 turnips
- 1 shallot
- 2 scallions
- 1 cucumber
- 1 red pepper
- ¼ oz. mint
- ¼ oz. parsley
- 1 lemon
- ½ cup Yoghurt

Method:

1. Cook quinoa and prepare turnip batter.
2. Heat 4 to 5 minutes to make crispy cakes.

TOASTED QUINOA STIR-FRY

Cooking Time: 30 minutes

Serving Size: 2

Calories: 510

Ingredients:

- ¾ cup quinoa
- 4 oz. shiitake mushrooms
- 1 tablespoon sesame seeds
- 3 oz. radish
- 2 teaspoon sesame oil
- 2 tablespoon tamari

Method:
1. Heat saucepan to make quinoa.
2. Slice vegetables and mushroom.
3. Cook and serve.

LOADED SWEET POTATO NACHOS

Cooking Time: 30 minutes

Serving Size: 2

Calories: 345

Ingredients:
- 1 lb. sweet potato
- 1 red onion
- 1 red bell pepper
- 0.25 oz. fresh cilantro
- 1 avocado
- 1 chipotle
- ⅓ cup vegan sour cream
- 1 package black beans

Method:
1. Make the chips and salsa.
2. Prepare the vegetables and chipotle.
3. Spice the beans and serve.

HAPPY PANCAKE

Cooking Time: 35 minutes

Serving Size: 2

Calories: 410

Ingredients:

- 2 scallions
- 3 oz. radish
- 1 garlic clove
- 2 tablespoon tamari
- 2 teaspoon sesame oil
- ⅔ cups of rice flour
- ¼ teaspoon turmeric
- 1 oz. pea shoots

Method:
1. Prepare vegetables and bake at 250°F for 20 minutes.
2. Tilt the skillet and fold pancakes to finish up.

HERBED BARLEY BOWL

Cooking Time: 35 minutes
Serving Size: 2
Calories: 670

Ingredients:
- ¾ cup barley
- 1 sugar
- 2 tablespoon apple cider vinegar
- 8 peppercorns
- 6 oz. mushroom
- 1 garlic clove
- 1 scallion
- ¼ cup pistachios
- 1 oz. arugula
- 1 lemon

Method:
1. Cut vegetables and mushrooms.
2. Cook barley, veggies and popcorn.

3. Add and mix ingredients to serve.

CAULIFLOWER SPARE RIBS

Cooking Time: 45 minutes

Serving Size: 2

Calories: 480

Ingredients:
- ¾ cup of rice
- 14 oz. cauliflower
- 2 garlic cloves
- Fresh ginger
- 1 scallion
- 6 oz. mustard greens
- 1 tablespoon ketchup
- 2 tablespoon sweet soy
- 1 teaspoon of rice wine vinegar
- 1 tablespoon cornstarch

Method:
1. Cook rice and cauliflower.
2. Make sauces and fry rice.
3. Mix rice with veggies and sauce to serve.

YAKI ONIGIRI

Cooking Time: 40 minutes

Serving Size: 2

Calories: 580

Ingredients:
- ½ cup of sushi rice

- 1 shallot
- 1 carrot
- Fresh ginger
- 2 tablespoon tamari
- 4 oz. radish
- 2 oz. peas
- 6 oz. cabbage
- 1 teaspoon miso paste
- 1 tablespoon vegan butter

Method:
1. Make the rice and prepare vegetables.
2. Shape Onigiri with vegetables.
3. Cook until brown and serve.

QUINOA FRIED RICE

Cooking Time: 35 minutes
Serving Size: 2
Calories: 640

Ingredients:
- 1 tofu
- ¼ teaspoon turmeric
- 1 onion
- 4 oz. carrot
- 1 scallion
- 2 teaspoon sesame oil
- ¾ cup quinoa
- 1 tablespoon tamari
- ½ cup green peas

Method:
1. Cook tofu and prepare vegetables.

2. Cook quinoa and mix with other ingredients to serve.

POTATO KOROKKE

Cooking Time: 45 minutes

Serving Size: 2

Calories: 345

Ingredients:
- 14 oz. potato
- 4 oz. mushrooms
- 2 shallots
- 3 tablespoon tamari
- 3 tablespoon rice wine vinegar
- ¾ cup of sushi rice
- 6 oz. snow peas
- 1 scallion
- 1 teaspoon sesame oil
- ½ cup all-purpose flour

Method:
1. Cook vegetables and sushi rice.
2. Prepare sauces and fry korokke (potato mashed).
3. Mix all ingredients to serve.

FAB CAKES

Cooking Time: 35 minutes

Serving Size: 2

Calories: 425

Ingredients:
- 1 jalapeño

- 1 package garbanzo beans
- 2 packets mustard
- 1 cup panko breadcrumbs
- 1 carrot

Method:
1. Chop all ingredients and mix to make the batter.
2. Make and fry cake on low heat.
3. Combine all and serve.

LATKES

Cooking Time: 45 minutes

Serving Size: 2

Calories: 530

Ingredients:
- 12 oz. potatoes
- 1 onion
- ¼ cup vegan mayonnaise
- 1 apple
- 1 tablespoon mustard
- 1 teaspoon mustard seeds
- 1 teaspoon sugar
- 2 tablespoon flour
- ⅓ cup vegan sour cream
- 4 oz. broccoli

Method:
1. Cook vegetables and fruits (latkes) for 10 to 15 minutes.
2. Make cream and fry latkes and serve.

TURMERIC-CARROT SOUP

Cooking Time: 35 minutes

Serving Size: 2

Calories: 270

Ingredients:
- 1 carrot
- 1 sweet potato
- 1 onion
- Fresh ginger
- Garlic
- 2 teaspoon turmeric
- 2 teaspoon curry powder
- 2 tablespoon vegetable broth powder
- 4 tablespoon coconut powder
- Fresh cilantro
- 2 oz. arugula

Method:
1. Chop and roast vegetables.
2. Let ingredients meld and make soup.
3. Blend and garnish the soup.

GAZPACHO VERDE

Cooking Time: 25 minutes

Serving Size: 2

Calories: 526

Ingredients:
- 1 lime
- Fresh cilantro
- 1 jalapeño
- 2 tomatillos

- 1 Granny Smith apple
- 1 cucumber
- 2 shallots
- Garlic
- 1 avocado
- 2 tablespoon vinegar
- 2 slices bread
- 1 tablespoon cornstarch

Method:
1. Prepare fruit and veggies and blend all.
2. Make an avocado toast and garnish with the mixture.

Conclusion

Eating a diet that is higher in plant sources and lower in animal foods will bring many beneficial effects, including weight loss or preservation and a reduced risk of heart disease and high blood pressure. If you want to move to a plant-based diet, you may begin by gradually decreasing the consumption of meat and dairy. Eating an entirely plant-based meal once a week, or exchanging one plant-based animal product at one, can be a fantastic starting point.

Plant-based diets can be healthier, including vegan diets, as long as they are balanced and nutritionally sufficient. A well-balanced, plant-based diet that focuses on whole grains, berries, legumes, nuts, vegetables, and seeds can provide health benefits if routinely followed. When you have got a taste for this delicious and nutritious plant-based diet, you have the resources to step it up to the next stage.

This book is an excellent choice if you want to learn how to cook whole-grain, plant-based food like a pro. If you are looking for a way to make cooking and grocery shopping simpler, check out the shopping list and 21-days meal plan. If you are having troubles in making your plant-based food, this book is the best chance for you to learn plant-based recipes and enhance your cooking skills.